T0316998

New Architecture in Wood

Marc Wilhelm Lennartz
Susanne Jacob-Freitag

NEW ARCHITECTURE IN WOOD

Forms and Structures

Birkhäuser
Basel

Preface

Human beings have been building wooden buildings since time immemorial. Indeed, in the Middle Ages, whole towns and cities were built from this natural raw material.

The current renaissance in timber construction began in the early 1990s – and there is no end in sight. Building with wood is booming. Worldwide, wood is the only renewable building material of any relevance that stores the carbon dioxide so crucial to the climate. In the age of climate change, greenhouse effect and energy policy U-turns, i.e. the shift to renewables, it is of central importance indeed. In the light of limited resources and the fact that timber can replace energy-intensive conventional building materials in many applications, this versatile material has become the very symbol of sustainable building.

In addition, the further systematic development of specialised production methods as well as digital design and fabrication techniques have raised timber construction to a new level of building without depleting resources. And in the German-speaking countries in particular, the significant R&D work being undertaken is regarded internationally as leading in this field. The results of these efforts have been incorporated in numerous product developments and industrialised forms of construction that have been used in initial applications, chiefly in Austria, Germany, Switzerland, and South Tyrol (Italy).

This book describes a number of highly disparate structures in order to demonstrate the diversity of modern timber construction and its many applications. Whether in the form of large-scale load-bearing structures or multi-storey buildings, or combined with other building materials, or in the context of integrated, socio-ecological urban planning, wood offers answers to many important questions that architects and urban planners have to tackle now and in the future.

Modern timber construction already represents a new humanistic and ecological architecture that could shape urban structures in the 21st century.

Quality was the trademark of Christoph & Unmack AG:
timber buildings were trial-assembled in huge sheds
prior to dispatch.

Looking for the origins of modern timber construction

Today's possibilities in the architectural and engineering design of timber structures of all kinds are inextricably linked with two pioneers of timber construction, namely Otto Hetzer (1846–1911) and Konrad Wachsmann (1901–1980). Whereas Hetzer made possible the construction of large-scale timber structures, Wachsmann saw the industrial possibilities of this ancient building material. Their life's work can be regarded as the basis of modern timber construction.

Industrialisation of the construction process

It was during his work in Lusatia in the 1920s that Konrad Wachsmann laid the foundation for an industrialised form of timber construction based on maximum prefabrication and systemisation. His methods and ideas, which can now be explored in the freshly restored Konrad Wachsmann House in Niesky, were way ahead of their time.

The architect Frei Otto described the œuvre of his colleague and friend as follows: 'I believe Wachsmann is the clearest thinker and philosopher in modern architecture. Like no other, he found a common denominator between technical innovation and beauty.'

The Central European regions of Upper and Lower Lusatia, like Silesia to the east, have a rich tradition of timber buildings. One of the most important protagonists of this legacy in modern times was born in Frankfurt an der Oder in 1901 – Konrad Wachsmann. Like the famous poet from the same town, Heinrich von Kleist, Wachsmann adhered to the maxim of a liberal intellectual education. All his life, Konrad Wachsmann was searching for the ideal material to realise and perfect his dream of an efficient, industrially machined and prefabricated modular form of construction. He defined the then new type of synthesis of technology and science as a 'new artistry in architecture'. Wachsmann pursued the spiritual ideals of the Bauhaus – and his aim was a comprehensive renewal of society. Nevertheless, he differed from Gropius and other Bauhaus proponents, who advocated a return to craftsmanship. Instead, he pinned his hopes on machine-made, technical components; for only these contained the space for the architectural utopias of the dreams he was contemplating and researching.

Mixing with the likes of Brecht, Lasker-Schüler and Grosz

Wachsmann did not complete his formal education and was apprenticed to a cabinetmaker. On the advice of his family he then moved to Berlin to attend the art college there. The courses at the college could not satisfy young Wachsmann's thirst for knowledge and experiencing life – but the Berlin of the 1920s had more to offer than just school lessons. The bohemian society that gathered in the Romanische Café fascinated him. This was where he could immerse himself in the world of artists and writers such as Bertolt Brecht, Else Lasker-Schüler, George Grosz, and Erika and Klaus Mann, and fully absorb the nascent all-embracing modern movement fed by the revolutionary spirit of the times. It was during this period that Wachsmann became convinced that architecture, too, and not just politics, art, literature, and music, was in need of a fundamental rethink. Art Nouveau had already lost its power to transform, and the good times of the preceding *Gründerzeit* era (literally the 'Founder Epoch') were over, as were the belligerent years under the Kaiser.

An age of revolutionary regeneration

In those days, most ordinary folk and the working classes lived in squalid blocks of flats, indeed, many of them in slum-like conditions. In addition, there was a shortage of housing. As far as Wachsmann was concerned, this was a situation just crying out for change. Furthermore, new objectivity, simplicity, and unobtrusiveness were on the agenda; bourgeois-aristocratic splendour and splash belonged to the past.

After completing his studies in architecture at the art academies in Dresden and Berlin, Wachsmann took the advice of his teacher Hans Poelzig and moved to Niesky in Saxony in 1926. Taken on as an architect by Christoph & Unmack AG, at that time the largest timber construction and engineering works in Europe, it was here that he quickly found what he had been seeking for so long. Not only was Christoph & Unmack way ahead of its time, it was also special in one significant respect. Contrary to the general preference for glass, steel, chromium, and reinforced concrete as building materials for the modern movement, the company based its industrially prefabricated building designs on a traditional building material – wood. The company's timber buildings were already being completely prefabricated by machine before being exported to countries across Europe, even by ship to Africa and North and South America. Wachsmann really thrived at the company, allowed himself to be inspired by the – for the times – incredible range of machinery available, and quickly rose to become chief architect at Christoph & Unmack. This post opened up further opportunities for him to promote his ideas and concepts regarding the maximum prefabrication and systemisation of industrialised forms of timber construction.

Diversity in unity with maximum variety

Wachsmann designed standardised panel systems, conceived precautionary measures that were ingenious in terms of their building technology, and reformed frame construction by employing new methods of structural calculation. In addition, he drafted new showhouse catalogues with a customer-centric, modular overall concept. Departing from the usual practice of presenting individual house types, his catalogues offered customers the chance to take part in a creative process to produce their own homes. Customers were able to assemble their own personal home according to their own ideas based on a set of prefabricated elements. The really clever part about Wachsmann's concept was being able to create maximum variety for an individual building despite the limited set of parts. Customers could design their dream homes themselves – from the 'typical Upper Lusatia style' to the functional appearance of the Bauhaus style – using a remarkable range of styles and designs.

Wachsmann later described his pioneering years in Niesky in these terms: 'It was the most decisive step in my life. In the woodworking shops of the factory, I was able to discover the world of machines, technology, the beginnings of industrialised building. Everything that came afterwards and happened in Berlin, New York, Tokyo, Chicago, London, Moscow, Paris, Rome, Zurich, or Warsaw all began in Niesky, a village founded by Moravian immigrants. It was in this wooden house factory that I discovered the way that led me to a turning point in construction.' (M. Grüning: *Der Wachsmann-Report,* Basel, 2001, p. 210)

Timber building centre of the world

Christoph & Unmack's range included, for example, building types in log construction or timber-frame buildings clad with boards, as well as panel and trussed forms of construction. The goal was the ongoing development of these forms of timber construction so that they could be manufactured in serial production. The firm's motto was 'Inexpensive, durable, thermally insulated, practical, modern.' They designed and built private- and public-sector buildings, hotels, churches, hospitals, gymnasiums, schools, railway stations, industrial sheds, and aircraft hangars, even transmission towers. Other renowned

B

C

A

D

E

A → Christoph & Unmack AG was already exporting prefabricated timber buildings to the rest of the world a century ago.

B → The architect Konrad Wachsmann recognised and developed the practices and opportunities of modern timber construction.

C → Pioneering architects and expatriates in America: Walter Gropius and Konrad Wachsmann.

D → Even today, visitors to Niesky can see almost 100 prefabricated timber buildings. Christoph & Unmack AG built these to house their workers. Moreover, these houses served as showhouses enabling new customers to inspect the various types of building.

E → The factory in Niesky reveals the scale that industrial timber construction had already reached at the start of the 20th century.

architects worked and experimented alongside Wachsmann at Christoph & Unmack, e.g. Prof. Albinmüller and Henry van de Velde.

In those days Niesky was the timber building centre of Europe, if not the world. Even today, visitors to this small town in the far south-eastern corner of Germany can see almost 100 prefabricated timber buildings dating from that period. Most of those are to be found in Neu-Ödernitz, an estate of timber houses where Christoph & Unmack appointed contractors to build 76 buildings containing 250 flats in panel construction. The workforce was delighted: 'We'll never want to swap our new timber homes for brick homes!' The timber buildings dating from those years are still occupied today. They are protected by the less stringent provisions of a preservation order that covers the area as a whole. The red clay tiles on the roofs and the brown colouring of the facades are among the things prescribed, but the buildings are nevertheless still in good condition.

National Socialism puts an end to modern timber buildings

The National Socialists' rise to power marked the beginning of the end for modern timber construction in Niesky. The directors of Christoph & Unmack at the time were only too happy to do the new government's bidding. As a result, a central planning committee was set up in Niesky which was responsible for building the wooden barracks at several thousand camps belonging to the extermination machinery of the German authorities in which millions of people were tortured and killed. The plans and ideas of this committee – with the help of timber contractors distributed across the territory of the German Reich – formed the basis for the design and construction of buildings for concentration and labour camps, along with field hospitals and military accommodation that could be quickly set up and quickly dismantled. Timber construction for non-military uses gradually lost its importance in those years.

After the war, Niesky provided reparations in the form of portable prefabricated timber buildings for a few years, but that spelled the end of industrialised timber buildings in Upper Lusatia. As for Wachsmann, following his successful years in Lusatia, his luck as an architect in Germany did not last very long, either. He did manage to study abroad, in Rome, but the Nazi dictatorship soon afterwards forced Wachsmann, with his Jewish background, to emigrate, first to Paris in 1938, then to the USA in 1941, helped by his friend Albert Einstein, for whom he had designed a summer cottage in Potsdam in 1929.

Emigration and post-war years

Wachsmann made a name for himself in the USA, primarily through the company he founded in New York together with Walter Gropius, the General Panel Corporation, and its 'Packaged House System', a sort of modular system for prefabricated timber construction. The two immigrants had their specific building components produced fully automatically – a new approach in those days. From 1949 onwards Wachsmann served as professor of building systems at the Institute of Design in Chicago, which had been founded by László Moholy-Nagy and Walter Gropius as the successor institution to the Bauhaus. In 1950 Ludwig Mies van der Rohe helped him to continue his research into the industrialisation of building as Director of the Department of Advanced Building Research at the Illinois Institute of Technology.

He had already devised a universal connection before emigrating, the Wachsmann node, which allowed standardised components to be assembled both vertically and horizontally. While in the USA, Wachsmann developed this connection further to create the 'Mobilar Structure Building System', a method of building large volume single-storey sheds without internal columns, e.g. aircraft hangars. He worked with a team of teachers and students – an integrative approach that also caused an international sensation – to develop what was at that time a totally new building system made up of steel tubes and connecting nodes. During the 1960s he continued his work as professor at the School of Architecture (University of Southern California) in Los Angeles.

After receiving many honours and being awarded internationally renowned architecture prizes, Konrad Wachsmann died in California in 1980. Although his mother, sister, and a nephew had died at the hands of the Nazis in a concentration camp, his express wish was to be buried in Germany, in his hometown of Frankfurt/Oder. The Academy of Arts in Berlin now manages the estate of this revolutionary and innovative architect.

Prefabrication and systemisation

Key areas of the modern timber construction of the 21st century can be traced back to the ideas and solutions of Konrad Wachsmann. The industrial prefabrication of all components in large batches with consistently high quality, the almost complete systemisation of timber construction, and the speeding-up of the whole construction process through a form of standardisation that still allows for diverse structures – all that had its origins in Niesky. That also applies to the well-developed quality management system, which included trial assemblies of timber buildings and other structures in huge sheds prior to sale and to being exported throughout the world. Incidentally, their load-bearing structures were made from Hetzer beams, which Otto Hetzer, the pioneer of engineered timber construction, had developed.

Structures and designs for engineered timber buildings

Historical events led to phases in which not only timber construction, but also engineered timber construction led a shadowy existence. Whereas wood, long established in construction, was virtually unrivalled as a building material up until the mid-19th century (many efficient timber building systems had been developed up to then which were already based on engineering methods and were very different from carpentry traditions), during the Industrial Revolution it started to lose favour from about 1850 onwards and was no longer the first choice for buildings. Throughout the world, building materials such as steel and concrete started to take over. So in the second half of the 19th century the pioneering structures were made from steel, or rather iron. Nevertheless, isolated engineering masterpieces were indeed built during this period, e.g. transmission towers, salt warehouses, and structures for the railways and the emerging airship industry.

The renewed upturn in engineered timber construction at the start of the 20th century can be primarily attributed to the invention of glued laminated timber by Otto Hetzer. In 1906 this master carpenter and entrepreneur from Weimar was granted a patent for his invention of curved glued timber components. Hetzer's basic idea was to take several boards and produce timber components in any length with any cross-section and with every conceivable curvature. The glued laminated timber components, known then as Hetzer beams, extended the constructional possibilities of engineered timber construction quite crucially. It was now possible to achieve load-carrying capacities that were inconceivable with solid timber. Spans of more than 40 metres were no longer a problem. That of course led to new structural forms. The invention of glued laminated timber is therefore regarded as the birth of modern engineered timber construction. Furthermore, at that time the new form of timber construction was almost 50 per cent cheaper than other forms of construction, especially reinforced concrete, and, consequently, also improved the competitiveness of timber construction.

So glued laminated timber started to be used for long-span structures. The first single-storey shed built using the Hetzer form of construction had a span of 43 metres. It was designed for German Railways by the architect Peter Behrens and was erected at the World Exposition in Brussels in 1910. Further large structures quickly followed. Switzerland built its share of these, including a dome for the main building at Zurich University (1911), industrial buildings, and numerous roofs over railway platforms. Indeed, Swiss Railways even published a corresponding recommendation, because the use of timber ruled out corrosion problems.

After the First World War, engineered timber construction became popular in Germany again. Although the fortunes of the company founded by Otto Hetzer began to decline in 1926, three years before the start of the global economic depression, his know-how didn't disappear with the company. From 1919 to 1922 Otto Alfred Hetzer, one of Otto Hetzer's sons, took charge of the renowned timber construction company based in Niesky, Christoph&Unmack, where he introduced his father's engineering legacy.

Major timber contractors also sprung up elsewhere in Germany. A wave of patent applications ensued and methods of connection were investigated scientifically and further developed. Building with glued laminated timber (glulam) had a major influence on timber construction in Germany and, over the decades, modern engineered building with timber evolved into the high-tech form of construction it is today.

New methods of connection and computer-assisted design

Methods of connection, but also new gluing techniques, are inextricably linked with engineered timber construction. Almost all the early engineered timber structures relied on handcrafted woodworking joints. However, the ever longer spans called for ever more efficient methods of connection. Many structural forms owed their existence to the new connections. Fastening and connecting techniques employing nails, steel dowels, special dowels, shaped steel plates, and threaded bars glued into drilled holes, along with the systematic investigation of finger joints, all played major roles in the further development of engineered timber construction.

The combination of glulam and cleverly designed load-bearing fasteners continues to open up new architectural opportunities. Spans of well over 100 metres are feasible these days. Of course, the structures are also influenced by the methods of analysis available. Trusses, beams, long-span arches, and trussed members are the preferred structural forms these days, again and again leading to new configurations that enrich engineered timber construction.

Computer-assisted design with 2D and 3D CAD tools, which enable fully automatically controlled CNC machining for the precise fabrication of glulam components with almost any dimensions, results in highly efficient forms of construction. Even components in double curvature can be produced without any problems.

More competitive than ever

Today, timber construction is in no way inferior to its rivals steel and concrete. In terms of aesthetic, functional, and even economic aspects, it can compete with conventional forms of construction. In several major European projects of recent years where tenders left the choice of material open and the clients made their decisions based purely on economic factors, timber was chosen over steel, for instance.

Modern engineered timber structures are high-tech assemblies offering unprecedented aesthetics. In addition, cleverly designed load-bearing structures are enormously efficient and light in weight at the same time, because wood exhibits a high strength for a low self-weight. Their particular forms have inspired many architects throughout the world to use this time-honoured building material.

The expertise of the German-speaking countries is unique in this field and in demand throughout the world. And systematic research and development places timber construction on the highest technical level, a fact demonstrated by the huge number of standardised and approved timber construction products and fasteners. Modern (engineered) timber construction has many facets and is sure to develop additional ones in the future. Further, the new awareness of the environment and the need to build energy-efficient, climate-neutral structures without depleting resources have awakened our interest in this unique form of construction more than ever before.

14

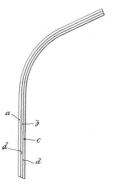

A

B

A → Otto Hetzer's patent of 1906

B → Otto Karl Friedrich Hetzer (Otto Hetzer sen.)

C → The International Hygiene Exhibition in Dresden in 1911 provided a chance to exhibit the Döcker gymnasium model with its parabolic arches made of glued Hetzer beams in the form of I-sections to save material. The authorities in Langerfeld, a suburb of Wuppertal, purchased the portable building and after the exhibition erected it at its current location, where it has served as a gymnasium and sports hall since 1912. It was refurbished in 2008.

D → Section through old gymnasium: Hetzer three-pin arches supporting a mansard roof

C

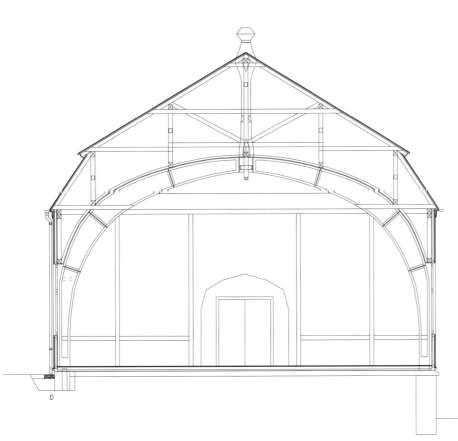

D

Public buildings

Conference hall made up of interlocking 'peep boxes'

The building for the World Intellectual Property Organisation (WIPO) in the heart of the UN quarter in Geneva has attracted plenty of attention. This highly asymmetric timber structure is designed as a plate structure made up of hollow box elements and trusses. Consequently, long spans could be achieved with little material. One special feature is the 35 metre long cantilevering section of the building.

Since September 2014 the World Intellectual Property Organisation (WIPO), founded in 1967, has had a new conference hall at its headquarters in Geneva. The 1600 m² building, clad in larch shingles and bronze-anodised sheet aluminium, seems to hover above the Place des Nations. Four interlocking, peep box-type timber tubes form a sculpted edifice. One of those tubes cantilevers 35 metres beyond the central base structure. According to the designers, it is the world's longest cantilever for an engineered timber structure of this kind.

The conference hall was built in the gardens of the WIPO headquarters between the two existing buildings dating from 1978 and 2011 and completes the ensemble.

Client's request: sustainability
The client wanted a sustainable building, so it was very quickly clear that timber would have to be used. The choice of material seemed sensible to the design team

and offered plenty of scope for complying with this stipulation. In addition, the primary energy requirement (grey energy) for building and operating the centre had to be kept to a minimum. However, timber with its low weight also exhibited clear advantages over concrete and steel when considering the building physics, the fire protection concept, and the high additional loads brought about by the safety and security aspects associated with a building of this category, and which had to be considered as accidental loads.

Furthermore, wood's acoustic properties and low thermal mass, and the building's fast heating or cooling response times associated with that were also seen as positive in the light of conference events with periods of use alternating with periods of inactivity.

The broad V-shaped plan form of the conference hall with its central 'stage' resembles that of an ancient Greek theatre. The 850 seats for delegates face the podium.

The search was on for a load-bearing structure for an asymmetric building

In the centre, the building, made up of four tapering timber tubes reminiscent of peep boxes, rests on a reinforced concrete base structure. The tubes spread out beyond the base in four directions. The longest cantilever is 35 metres, the second-longest 17 metres; these two tubes are identical apart from their lengths.

The structural engineers initially developed a plate structure in the form of self-supporting, bending- and torsion-resistant tubes in cross-laminated timber (CLT) to suit this highly asymmetric configuration with constantly changing heights and widths. They wanted to explore the advantages of CLT as a material capable of carrying biaxial loads, but also comply with the architects' requirement for incorporating a maximum amount of timber.

However, with suspended floors spanning up to 20 or 28 metres, a pure plate structure (i.e. in-plane-loaded structure) could only carry the tensile and compressive stresses distributed globally over the plates in the longitudinal direction, but not the local bending stresses in the transverse direction, e.g. due to snow on the roof or occupied rows of seats on the floor. To carry those loads, further members transverse to the direction of the cantilever would be necessary. Therefore, the engineers modified the simple solid timber solution and worked out various alternatives using resolved and assembled designs with ribs for the transverse load-carrying capacity. In the end they chose hollow boxes.

With a total depth of 1.50 metres, ribs made of 18 centimetre wide Kerto-S every 1.25 metres were attached via shear-resistant connections to the top and bottom panels made from 15 centimetre thick CLT to create a plate structure that could carry all the loads.

More steel in timber construction to keep within budget

A consortium set up specially for the project then reworked this design once again to find a more cost-effective variation, which, however, reduced the amount of timber in the load-bearing structure. They replaced the CLT and the Kerto in the hollow boxes with glued laminated timber and reduced the depth to 1.20 metres. Trusses with cladding attached using shear-resistant fixings were selected for the sides of the cantilevering tubes. These changes to create uniaxial load-carrying components now called for the inclusion of additional steel beams and columns. This was the solution that was chosen to be built.

Load-bearing structure on bridge bearings

The greatest challenges were the stiffness and deformation of the tube cantilevering 35 metres and the supports for the building – the latter mainly because the options for positioning the supports on the existing substructure were limited. Therefore, the building is anchored to the reinforced concrete base structure at 18 points. In order to be able to transfer the forces safely to the substructure – forces due to dead, imposed, wind, and special loads that result from the use of the building (all with different magnitudes and acting in different directions) –, the structural engineers installed bearings that are common in bridge-building (also partly because the loads of up to 1000 tonnes are similar to those of bridges).

Spherical bearings guarantee a controlled load transfer between superstructure and substructure, and permit tilting movements to all sides plus displacements of the superstructure. Vertical and horizontal forces are transferred directly to the base structure; rotations are accommodated by the movable spherical part and a concave base section to the bearing.

The challenge of the 'security-specific special load'

Under vertical loading, the entire building reacts like a propped cantilever. These loads are made up of the dead loads, the imposed load for the conference hall ($4\,kN/m^2$), the imposed load for other areas ($2\,kN/m^2$), and the snow load ($0.8\,kN/m^2$). The ensuing moment at the cantilever support presented the engineers with a tricky task due to the enormous cantilever of 35 metres.

They resolved the moment into a tension-compression couple and tied it back to the substructure with steel posts and diagonals via the two supports beneath the end bay of the truss. The highest tensile force that had to be accommodated was 200 tonnes! For stability, the open front end of this tube has a rigid frame with steel X-bracing (as do the windows in the ends of the other three tubes). So some of the loads of the 35 metre long cantilever on one side could be transferred to the 17 metre truss cantilever on the other side and thus improve the stiffness of the overall system.

One particular challenge for the design of the load-bearing structure was how to deal with the horizontal forces. Even just the 'security-specific special load' was about ten times the size of the wind load. Together with the earthquake load, the horizontal loads were many times greater than customary loads. To accommodate the ensuing transverse and torsional forces, transverse bulkheads were installed in and between the hollow boxes.

FEM for determining forces and deformations

The building was modelled in three dimensions with the help of the finite element method (FEM) and simulated as a spatial structure. Consequently, it was possible to determine the forces and deformations and design all the structural members. The interaction of the hollow box elements of the floors and walls (i.e. the timber-clad

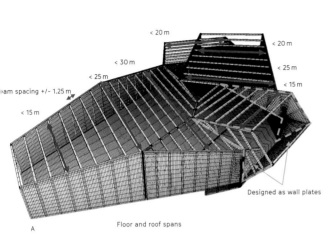

< 20 m

< 20 m

< 30 m

< 25 m

< 25 m

< 15 m

»am spacing +/- 1.25 m

< 15 m

Designed as wall plates

A

Floor and roof spans

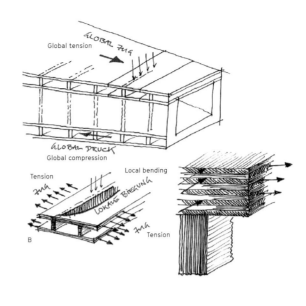

Global tension

GLOBAL ZUG

GLOBAL DRUCK
Global compression

Tension

Local bending

ZUG

LOKALE BIEGUNG

B

ZUG

Tension

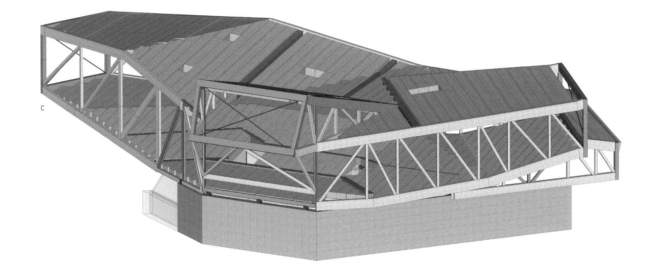

C

A → The roof and floor spans input into the 3D computer model of the structural variation 'hollow box made of CLT and Kerto ribs'.

B → Principle for carrying loads in two directions with hollow boxes made of CLT

C → Instead of CLT hollow boxes everywhere, in the end the design team chose glulam hollow boxes for the floors, walls, and trusses. That resulted in the use of more steel components.

D → Daylight enters through the huge, skyward-facing window to illuminate the podium in the conference hall.

D

trusses), all linked to form plates and frames, ensures the stability of the building.

Shear-resistant connections turn hollow boxes into plates

The 1.25 metre wide and 1.20 metre deep hollow box elements (panels and ribs: d=10 cm) of the roof surfaces span up to 28 metres, the 90 centimetre deep floor elements up to 20 metres. They were positioned by crane at a spacing of 2.50 metres between the 50 centimetre thick and up to 11.50 metre high wall plates, or rather between the top and bottom chords of the trusses.

Glued laminated timber edge beams with integral zip-type steel nib strips close off the tops of the walls, which are likewise hollow boxes made from 10 centimetre thick glulam panels and 30 centimetre deep glulam ribs. These function as support brackets for the hollow boxes of the floors.

The nib strips accommodate the panel edges to the hollow boxes top and bottom and hold them rigidly. The panel edges were cut accurately for this purpose. Screw fixings are used at the junctions between walls and floors and thus form the rigid frames or tube segments. Transverse glulam bulkheads are installed between the hollow boxes. They were able to be inserted exactly from above via the cut-outs in the projecting panels of the hollow boxes and interlocked with them. Further glulam panels close off the gaps top and bottom. Screwed to the transverse bulkheads and the adjacent hollow boxes,

they link the elements to form plates and hence the frames to form torsion-resistant tubes.

Unique in terms of geometry and strength

Every hollow box in the building has a different length and support geometry; and the glulam ribs to the walls and floors have different depths. Depending on the spans, however, they also have different strengths. The suspended floor elements were also fabricated with a camber, which was sized such that the loads of the hollow boxes would pull them horizontal after erection. The size of the camber is also specific to each beam. Therefore, every element is a one-off.

Precise planning with 3D CAD

The planning and fabrication of the glued laminated timber elements were carried out with a 3D computer model into which all the geometries as well as cut-outs for connecting plates and steel fasteners plus ventilation outlets had been input accurately. This model formed the basis for the CNC machining of all timber and steel components. The factory-prefabricated glulam hollow box elements were comparatively light and therefore easy to erect by crane. Only the erection of the long cantilever required falsework: the lower suspended floor and the hollow box walls, supplemented by the trusses, were installed and joined to the roof elements to form a huge tube. Only after being completed the structural system functions as intended. sjf

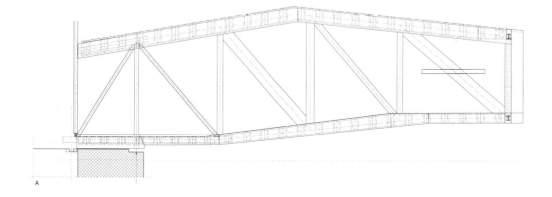

A → The moment from the 35 metre long cantilever is resolved into a tension-compression couple and transferred to the substructure in the end bay.

B → The truss on the other side is, structurally, a beam on two supports with a 17 metre cantilever.

C → Lifting a factory-prefabricated hollow box beam

D → Installing a transverse bulkhead between the hollow boxes to accommodate torsional forces

E → The steel nibs and edge cut-outs fit together like a puzzle. After installing the transverse bulkheads, glulam panels close off the gaps between the hollow boxes.

C

D

E

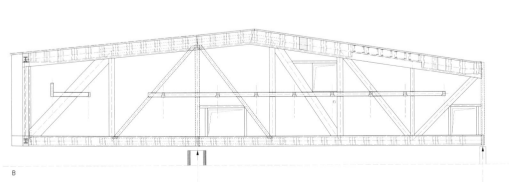

B

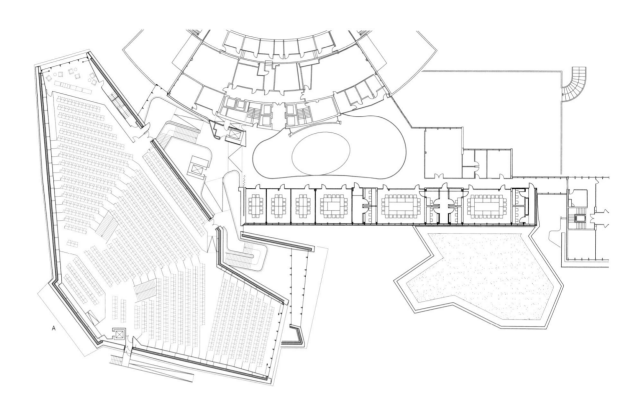

A

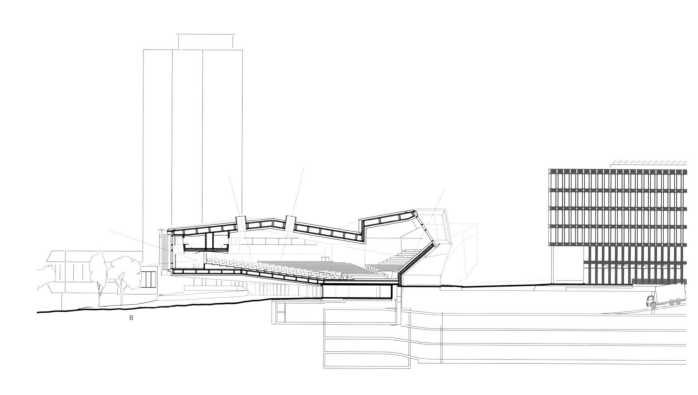

B

A → Floor plan

B → Section: one wing of the conference hall cantilevers 35 metres over the Place des Nations.

C → The bold architecture of this timber structure is convincing; compact and essentially closed, its tapering, cantilevering wings seem to hover above the Place des Nations, contrasting with the two existing glass/steel/concrete buildings of the WIPO complex.

C

<u>Project</u> WIPO conference hall (OMPI – Organisation Mondiale de la Propriété Intellectuelle; WIPO – World Intellectual Property Organisation) in Geneva, www.wipo.int

<u>Form of construction</u> Engineered timber structure

<u>Construction period</u> August 2011 to September 2014

<u>Costs</u> not specified

<u>Gross floor area</u> 7700 m²

<u>Gross enclosed volume</u> 29 000 m³

<u>Client</u> World Intellectual Property Organization (WIPO), 1211 Geneva, Switzerland, www.wipo.int

<u>Architecture</u> Behnisch Architekten, 70197 Stuttgart, Germany, www.behnisch.com

<u>Project supervision</u> Atelier Coplan, 1700 Fribourg, Switzerland, www.atelier-coplan.ch

<u>Project management</u> Burckhardt+Partner AG, 1227 Carouge GE, Switzerland, www.burckhardtpartner.ch

<u>Structural engineering, timber conceptual design</u> schlaich, bergermann und partner, 70197 Stuttgart, Germany, www.sbp.de; T Ingénierie SA, 1211 Geneva, Switzerland, www.t-ingenierie.com

<u>Structural engineering, reinforced concrete</u> Erricos Lygdopoulos, 1204 Geneva, Switzerland

<u>Structural engineering, detailed design & erection of timber</u> Bois OMPI consortium: Charpente Concept SA, 1258 Perly, Switzerland, www.charpente-concept.com; SJB Kempter + Fitze AG, 9101 Herisau, Switzerland, www.sjb.ch; JPF-Ducret SA, 1630 Bulle 1, Switzerland, www.jpf-ducret.ch; Dasta Charpentes Bois SA, 1228 Plan-les-Ouates, Switzerland, www.dasta.ch

<u>Climate consultants / Building services</u>
Transsolar Energietechnik GmbH, 70563 Stuttgart, Germany, www.transsolar.com; Sorane SA, 1024 Ecublens, Switzerland, www.sorane.ch; Riedweg & Gendre SA, 1227 Carouge, Switzerland, www.rgsa.ch

<u>Facade consultants</u> Emmer Pfenninger Partner AG, 4142 Münchenstein, Switzerland, www.eppag.ch

<u>Wooden shingles supplier</u> Theo Ott, 83404 Ainring-Hammerau, Germany, www.holzschindeln.de; consultant for wooden shingles facade: Baeriswyl AG, 3186 Düdingen, Switzerland, www.baeriswyl-ag.ch

<u>Consultant for glass facade & roof</u> Sottas SA, 1630 Bulle, Switzerland, www.sottas.ch

<u>Acoustics</u> Muller-BBM, 82152 Planegg, Germany, www.muellerbbm.de

<u>Bearings</u> Mageba SA, 8180 Bülach, Switzerland www.mageba.ch

<u>Quantity of timber used</u> 2100 m³ glulam

<u>Carbon (C) content</u> 525 t

<u>Sequestered CO_2</u> 1924 t

<u>Project details</u>
3595 m² (1280 m³) hollow boxes, thereof 395 m³ external wall elements
2745 m² panels with d = 10 cm
430 m³ glulam for trusses
2370 m² shingles
Longest cantilever: 35 m
Height of walls: 11.50 m

<u>Further information</u>
Time-lapse film of construction:
http://tinyurl.com/mc58ehc
(go to "Morphing of the construction")

A dome resembling a covering of foliage

The elephant house at Zurich Zoo is much more than just a home for ten Asian elephants. With its unusual roof and facade structure, it is an attraction in itself. It is primarily the multi-layer composite cross-section of the net-like dome that represents a pioneering construction feat and sets new standards when it comes to turning an initial vision into a structural engineering solution. The structure was awarded the Ulrich Finsterwalder Structural Engineering Award 2015.

Following three years of construction, June 2014 saw the opening of the new Kaeng-Krachan Elephant Park at Zurich Zoo. With a total area of about 11 000 m², the compound provides a home for up to ten Asian elephants and is six times larger than the original facility dating from the 1970s. An international architectural competition for the new facility was launched in 2008. The aim of the competition was to create a top-quality home for the elephants which would be better than any other in the world.

The winning design conceived the elephant park as a spacious landscape with external enclosures and dense vegetation in the visitor areas. And in the middle of all this the construction highlight, i.e. the elephant house. The architects' idea was to recreate the elephants' natural habitat in Thailand. The shallow dome had to form part of the landscape and look like a covering of foliage.

Multi-layer lightweight construction for net-like dome
The roughly 80 metre diameter, 6800 m² free-form timber roof shell spans over the internal enclosure like a huge net. In total, 271 rooflights are integrated in the timber shell, each one in the form of a transparent air-filled cushion made of UV-permeable ETFE foil. Together, they ensure that plenty of daylight reaches the interior

Interior view showing the roof shell with its rooflights. There are no pipes or cables on the soffit of the net-type roof. The light-permeable membranes of the air-filled cushions allow plants to grow inside the building.

beneath the shell – 18 metres high at its highest point. The realisation of this perforated, very shallow roof shell (span/rise ratio = 8:1) called for the development of a highly efficient, weight-saving design. To deal with this task, the structural engineers managed to devise a multi-layer nailed and screwed, and hence linear elastic, composite cross-section that could be assembled on site.

The specification called for a smooth soffit to the dome functioning as a structural lining and unencumbered by pipes or cables. The proportion of openings, amounting to about 35 per cent, was very important because the animals and plants below need ample sunlight, or rather UV light. The rooflights are not positioned randomly. Instead, they fit in with the structural options that the model of the shell permits. Each rooflight has a totally different geometry and the largest ones measure 40 m².

The elephant house is designed as a reinforced concrete ring. The shape of the undulating edge to the roof depends on the particular functions underneath. The heights and design of the supporting structure were influenced by the 'impact and attack heights' of the elephants (6 tonnes at a height of 2.5 metres), the sight-lines between internal and external areas for visitors, and the door clearances required.

Poor subsoil in some areas

The site is located on a slope, which is why the building and its basement disappear into the hill on one side and the ground slab lies on rock. On the valley side, how-ever, where the separate roof supports are located, the ground had little bearing capacity and was vulnerable to settlement. Anchoring back to the underlying rock was therefore essential.

The difficult subsoil conditions called for a lightweight structure and so timber was considered. The timber shell without any intermediate supports is bounded by a reinforced concrete ring beam and prestressed by the prestressing forces of the steel cables (up to 120 metres long) in the beam. The lowest points of the ring beam are the five support zones. These transfer the forces from the roof to the four groups of columns and the curving external wall around the stalls, which accounts for about one-third of the perimeter of the building and constitutes a continuous linear support.

To resist the horizontal thrust of the shell at the lowest points, the supports on the valley side are tied back to the bedrock with prestressed ground anchors. The local support zones are resolved into individual cantile-vering wall plates. This load-bearing structure merges with the slats of the timber facade to form a dynamic system that creates fluid transitions between the areas of concentrated load transfer and the intermediate transparent facade sections.

The complexity of the roof shell is matched by that of the facade. The connections between the cranked glulam facade posts and the edge of the roof had to be designed in such a way that they could accommodate vertical deformations amounting to tens of centimetres.

Ring beam in double curvature

The main difference between this dome and a conven-tional dome design is that the roof shell to the elephant house is not supported at one level. It was therefore impossible to create a tension ring that could resist the horizontal thrust, which would have simplified the foundations considerably. Instead, the perimeter of the roof is more like a beam subjected to biaxial bending – because in order to be able to prestress the ring beam against the shell, the steel cables constantly change their position within the cross-section, from top to bottom depending on whether they are in the 'crest' or the 'valley' of the beam. Every point of inflexion is in front of a support, which leads to bending about the weak axis as well.

The solution: a multi-layer composite cross-section

In structural terms, the roof functions as a shell with stiffening 'rays'. To achieve this, the engineers devised a multi-layer cross-section with a flexible combination of cross-laminated timber (CLT) boards and solid structural timber sections.

Three layers of CLT, each 8 centimetres thick, together form the 24 centimetre thick primary structure. This primary structure consists of a total of 600 individual pieces that are fitted together like a puzzle with half a million nails. Screwed on top of these around the open-ings are three-part solid timber ribs that strengthen the timber shell; along the main 'rays' they are positioned between the openings. The whole roof is insulated with 24 centimetre thick mineral wool. A 57 millimetre thick Kerto Q panel forms the top chord to the 54 centimetre deep structural cross-section.

Above this structure, timber blocks are attached so that there is a space for services, a sort of raised access floor. The blocks are arranged in such a way that they also help to position the pairs of criss-crossing screws driven home at 45 degrees.

Additional two-part solid timber ribs and wood-based panels form the insulating layer. The upper sheathing, a 28 millimetre thick wood-cement particleboard, trans-fers the forces tangential to the roof surface from the framing sections of the air-filled cushions to the structure below.

As the main 'rays' had to be fabricated as flexible composite cross-sections, relatively large deformations occur. These have been estimated to be on an order of

A → The elephant house with its striking roof is situated in the middle of the elephant park.

B → Example of the 'flattened', or rather developed, cutting pattern for the panel strips

C → Section through elephant house showing geology. There is a layer of sand and a compacted earth-sand mix both inside and outside. The very shallow roof shell leads to horizontal forces of up to 500 tonnes acting on the individual supports.

D → Reinforced concrete piers and ring beam showing the positions of the prestressing cables

E → The shell model with load-bearing 'ray' arches generated using the finite element method (FEM). Polygonal meshes that subdivide the mathematically precise geometrical areas into calculable individual pieces form the starting point for every FEM analysis.

29

A

B

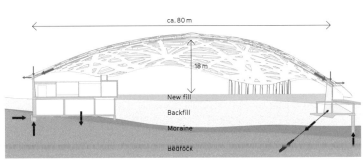

ca. 80 m

18 m

New fill

Backfill

Moraine

Bedrock

C

E

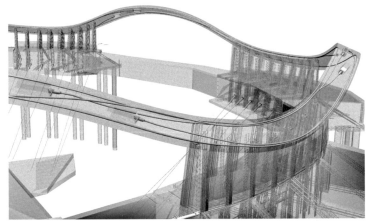

D

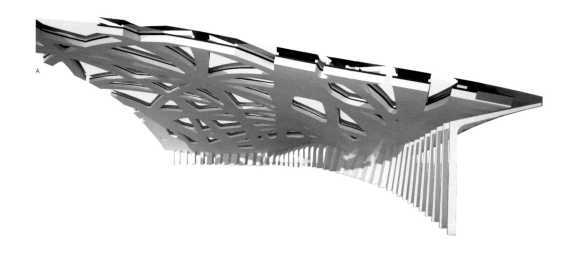

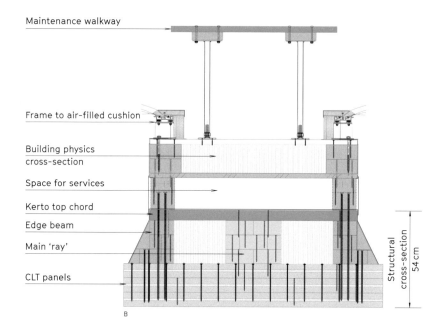

Maintenance walkway

Frame to air-filled cushion

Building physics
cross-section

Space for services

Kerto top chord

Edge beam

Main 'ray'

CLT panels

Structural
cross-section
54 cm

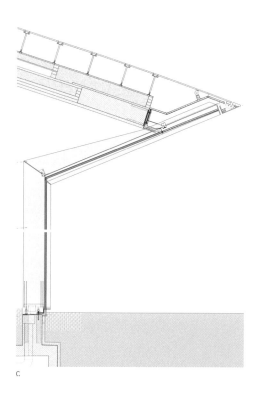

A → Perspective view

B → Typical section; the dowel-type fasteners ensure
the necessary ductility and robustness.

C → Typical section showing reinforced concrete
ring beam, fixed-based glulam facade posts, and
cantilevering beam (with pinned connection at
ring beam)

magnitude compatible with conventional timber structures (l/300). The air-filled cushions therefore had to be designed in such a way that they could be prefabricated but so the fixing of the perimeter framing to the supporting structure could compensate for tolerances of 2–3 centimetres.

The topmost sheathing is finished with a layer of waterproofing material. The maintenance level is raised 50 centimetres clear of that. The final depth of the roof is about 90 centimetres (excluding maintenance walkway).

Some 15 000 screws for a secure rustproof connection

Transferring the forces between the three orthotropic layers of the roof shell called for nailing over the entire area. Actually, the 24 centimetre thick primary structure on its own would have been sufficient to carry the self-weight of the shell. However, in order to achieve the necessary flexural rigidity required to cope with asymmetric loading cases such as wind or snow, three edge beams were needed around the rooflights as well as the panel forming the top chord. Together, they form a spatial honeycomb structure.

Special screws up to 85 centimetres long were needed to transfer the shear forces between the Kerto panels forming the top chord and the roof shell.

Precise design data thanks to automated numerical models

The construction solution for the roof shell is the result of an iterative form-finding procedure using parametric software. The aim of the parametric 3D model was to integrate the extensive architectural and engineering boundary conditions in the programmes from the first draft design phase onwards so that it would be possible to generate and verify the complete 3D geometry automatically. This model was required because it was necessary to reproduce the anisotropic properties of the wood in the multi-layer, flexible composite section with sufficient accuracy.

Several programmes were needed to create the parametric 3D model. The definitions of the beams, nodes, and edges projected onto plan plus the distribution of the nodes over the entire model with a selectable density were incorporated in the model, initially as 2D information. Afterwards, the entire model was deformed in three dimensions while retaining the positions of the openings.

As well as the geometry, it was also possible to import component parameters as well as all the structural system parameters defined by the engineers, e.g. spring supports and combinations, into the 3D model. It was therefore possible to check the output of every subprogrammes and carry out any modifications necessary or deal with exceptions manually. So at every stage it was possible to integrate the specific requirements or define them more precisely or modify them.

Cutting panels to size for double-curvature roof geometry

The free-form 3D surface had to be converted into flat 2D strips for the production and erection of the double-curvature roof shell. In order to develop the structural action of the shell, the panel strips had to be as large as possible. Taking into account the maximum production and transport dimensions, each of the three layers of cross-laminated timber were developed with the help of a software module programmed for this task. They measure up to 3.4×12 metres in size. The definition of the panel joints was carried out according to the structural requirements. The pattern of the joints in the bottom layer can be seen on the soffit of the shell. The patterns of the joints in all three layers were lined up so it was possible to mark the lines of the second layer on top of the first.

There are about 200 panels in each layer. Every panel is unique and required a file in machine code plus a fabrication drawing. So nothing else could stand in the way of automated panel production.

First layer over the entire area, second and third with openings

The double-curvature roof to the elephant house was erected on temporary timber ribs. To do this, ribs were attached to scaffolding falsework erected over the entire area to reproduce the negative form of the roof shell. The three layers of CLT boards forming the primary structure were laid on this falsework. Each layer was turned through 60 degrees with respect to the previous one supported on the ribs, giving the roof its shape so that the principal load-bearing direction of each layer points towards one support area.

To simplify erection on site, the structural engineers chose the panel construction so that it could be easily bent about two axes. The panel self-weight was almost sufficient in itself to give them the right form when laid on the falsework.

For reasons of stability, the first layer did not have any openings when first erected, whereas the openings for the rooflights had already been cut in the second layer. To position the second layer, the openings had been marked on the first layer. The openings in the third layer were factory-cut and this layer served as a template for the rooflights. Chainsaws were used to cut through all three layers cleanly after installing all fixings.

Ring beam concrete not poured until roof shell in place

The designers formed the transition to the ring beam in such a way that the first layer could be used directly as formwork. The top-side formwork needed when using self-compacting concrete was also integrated into the load-bearing structure. This method created a fixed support for the roof shell at the ring beam, which was not cast until the roof shell had been erected. Upon completing the ring beam, the roof became self-supporting and the falsework could be taken down.

Timber blocks forming space for services also help to position and install screws

The erection of the edge beams and main 'rays' followed according to an exact layout drawing, plus the formation of the space for services with timber blocks. The timber blocks were laid out in such a way that they could be

used to help position the pairs of screws driven home at 45 degrees which 'tie together' the multi-layer composite structural cross-section. The diagonal full-thread screws form a sort of truss in the flexible composite construction so that the necessary flexural rigidity is achieved.

The blocks prescribe the number, position and installation direction of the screws and also provide good guidance for the 85 centimetre long fasteners. They simplified erection considerably.

The behaviour of the seven-part composite cross-section is similar in tension and compression. Owing to the substantial flexibility in the joints, however, the flexural rigidity is only about 30 per cent of that of a comparable cross-section with rigid connections. sjf

A

B

C

D

A → Once the CLT boards had been nailed together, chainsaws were used to cut the openings in the first layer and trim those in the second layer to size.

B → A layer of laminated veneer lumber (LVL) was added above the finished roof shell to provide a maintenance walkway.

C → Erecting the edge beams and main 'rays'

D → The second and third layers were supplied with factory-cut openings for the rooflights.

E → 3D schematic exploded view of the overlapping principle of the edge beams in the various layers. At the 'ray' joints, only every second member is continuous in each direction. Diagonal WR-T screws (top) and other SFS screw types (WT-T, WS-T and composite screw VB) connect the three layers of cross-laminated timber making up the roof shell.

F → The timber blocks forming the space for services also helped to position and guide the 85 centimetre long WR-T special screws installed at 45 degrees.

G → This aerial view shows the impressive network structure of the large roof shell.

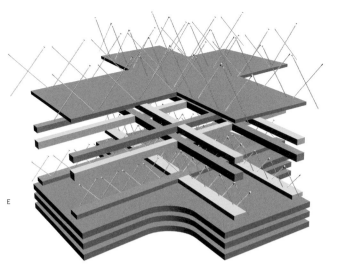

E

F

Project Elephant house, Zurich Zoo, www.zoo.ch

Form of construction Engineered timber construction on reinforced concrete supporting structure

Construction period May 2011 to May 2014

Costs approx. SFr 41 million

Enclosed volume 68 000 m³

Client Zoo Zürich AG, 8044 Zurich, Switzerland, www.zoo.ch

Overall management cga – consulting group aeberhard gmbh, 8400 Winterthur, Switzerland, www.cgateam.ch; BGS & Partner Architekten AG, 8640 Rapperswil, Switzerland, www.bgs-architekten.ch

Architecture Markus Schietsch Architekten GmbH, 8004 Zurich, Switzerland, www.markusschietsch.com

Site management Fischer Architekten AG, 8045 Zurich, Switzerland (site co-management, detailed design of stalls/lodge), www.fischer-architekten.ch; BGS & Partner Architekten AG, 8640 Rapperswil, Switzerland, www.bgs-architekten.ch

Landscape architecture Lorenz Eugster Landschaftsarchitektur und Städtebau GmbH, 8004 Zurich, Switzerland, www.lorenzeugster.ch; vetschpartner Landschaftsarchitekten AG, 8001 Zurich, Switzerland, www.vetschpartner.ch

Structural & facade engineering, site management for timber construction / building envelope Walt + Galmarini AG, 8008 Zurich, Switzerland, www.waltgalmarini.com

Building services engineers Tri Air Consulting AG, 8645 Jona, Switzerland, www.triair.ch

Electrical engineers Schmidiger + Rosasco AG, 8050 Zurich, Switzerland, www.srzh.ch

Parametric design Kaulquappe GmbH, 8004 Zurich, Switzerland, www.kaulquappe.net

Erection of timber structure 'Elefantenpark Holzbau' consortium: Implenia Schweiz AG Holzbau, 8050 Zurich, Switzerland, www.implenia.com; STRABAG AG Holzbau, 8315 Lindau, Switzerland, www.strabag.com

Panel production & facade design MERK Timber GmbH, Züblin Holz-ingenieurbau, 86551 Aichach, Germany, www.merk.de

Fasteners (screws) SFS intec AG, 9435 Heerbrugg, Switzerland, www.sfsintec.biz

Air-filled cushions Vector Foiltec GmbH, 28717 Bremen, Germany, www.vector-foiltec.com

Quantity of timber used 14 000 m² CLT boards (500 t timber) in 600 separate pieces 400 m³ edge beams / main 'rays' (150 t solid structural timber); 3500 m² Kerto top-chord panels (100 t)

Quantity of timber used 2041 m³

Carbon (C) content 510.25 t

Sequestered CO_2 1871 t

G

Commercial buildings

Shopping below a giant wave

The 'G3 Shopping Resort', a huge shopping mall in Gerasdorf on the outskirts of Vienna, opened its doors for the first time in October 2012. Particularly conspicuous is the long wavy roof which is made up of cross-laminated timber panels in different sizes and bent to different forms.

The 'G3' in the name symbolises the fact that there are three large building complexes in Gerasdorf positioned around a central car park: a shopping centre, a specialist retail centre, and a DIY store. And the 'Resort' in the name is intended to suggest to visitors that this is an especially pleasant place for relaxing and spending their time.

The shopping centre is the largest of the three buildings. It is covered by a boomerang-shaped timber roof that is 740 metres long and 70 to 140 metres wide, with an area of 58 000 m². Resembling a giant wave, the form of the roof is just as impressive as its dimensions. It consists of curved glued laminated timber beams supporting the roof decking of cross-laminated timber (CLT) panels, all supported on about 800 columns, some of which are 20 metres high. The shops along the sides of the mall have conventional flat roofs, also in timber.

The architects and structural engineers worked together to conceive the roof structure. The glulam beams of the 'giant wave' are positioned on the building grid-lines 8 metres apart and form the primary structure together with the fixed-base steel and reinforced concrete columns. The roof plate on top of the beams constitutes the secondary structure bracing the entire building. Owing to the considerable variation in form, which also has to accommodate two large teardrop-shaped openings, three different structural systems were needed:

- In the long end sections the glulam beams slope inwards, are connected in the middle via special steel nodes, and are supported on reinforced concrete external columns and Y-shaped steel central columns.
- In the middle of the building, three-part glulam beams – the longest parts are up to 80 metres long – span from the outer reinforced concrete columns over two internal steel 'tree' columns, each with four 'branches'. Steel nodes connect the three-part beams rigidly by means of steel plates let into the timber with elongated holes for the steel dowels so that changes in length can be accommodated without restraint.
- In the areas with the teardrop-shaped openings, simply supported glulam beams are used, spanning between reinforced concrete columns.

In addition, there are transverse beams that function as tension and compression members. These are positioned along the edge of the roof on the axes of the reinforced concrete columns and in the middle of the roof aligned with the tops of the columns.

Roof plate assembled from unique panels
The undulating roof form curving in all directions posed certain challenges for the design team at Graf-Holztechnik. Cross-laminated timber is easy to bend up to a certain point and so rounded forms are possible. However, managing to curve the roof surface in two

The roof to the mall is 740 metres long and 80 metres wide at its widest point, the main entrance. It covers the 'retailing paradise' like a giant wave.

A

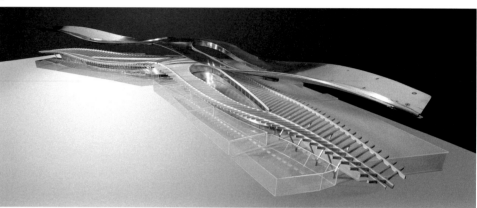

B

C

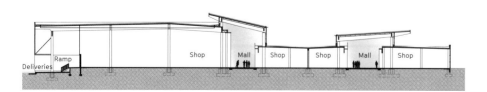

D

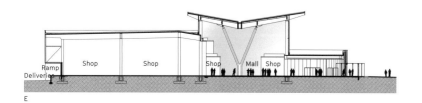

E

A → Aerial view of the curving, wave-shaped timber roof shell during construction; the difference in height at the middle is about 8 metres.

B → Model of mall roof with longitudinal and transverse members forming primary structure and CLT roof plate (here in aluminium) as secondary structure

C → Spacious and airy – the shopping mall after completion

D → Section through the areas with the droplet-shaped roof openings

E → Section through building in long end sections

directions called for careful planning with respect to the detailing of the elements, the arrangement of the joints between panels, and the connections between them to form a plate.

The 3D design software cadwork was used to 'design' every panel, because almost every one of them is unique. Although most of the panels are 16 metres long – spanning two bays – and 3 metres wide and thus identical in terms of their plan dimensions, the thickness required from the structural engineering viewpoint had to be calculated for each panel separately in order to end up with a design that was as slim and economic as possible. The upshot of that was thirteen different panel thicknesses ranging from 9.4 to 24 centimetres.

During erection, the individual panels were laid like sheet materials and offset by half a panel length each time. For the 16 metre long panels, the curvature of the roof surface resulted in height differences of up to one metre measured across the diagonal from lowest to highest corner. In addition, owing to the unequal curvatures of the roof, every panel twists slightly differently. In some instances this geometry led to gaps up to 2 centimetres wide between the longitudinal edges of neighbouring panels. As it was still possible to form a plate like this, the opening and closing of the joints was accepted, which saved elaborate, costly machining of the panel edges. A suspended ceiling ensures that the joints are not visible from underneath.

Shear connectors, nails, screws, and flange head screws ensure plate action

The panels were joined via shear connectors made from 25 millimetre thick OSB strips fitted on top of the panels. The site crews laid the strips in corresponding recesses factory-cut in the edges of the panels and nailed them to the cross-laminated timber panels to create a shear-resistant connection. The panels were also screwed to the glulam beams along the joints.

In addition, the longitudinal sides of the panels are held together with flange head screws in order to harmonise the different 'sags' of the CLT panels between the glulam beams and create a stable whole.

With different thicknesses of CLT panels being used, the soffit was flush after erection but the level of the upper surface changed from panel to panel. In order to compensate for this, different thicknesses of thermal insulation were laid to suit the panels below.

A cold-applied self-adhesive vapour barrier was laid between the timber roof and the insulation. On top of the insulation there is merely a layer of PVC-free FPO waterproof sheeting.

Brief preparation time and demanding logistics

The big challenge for the timber contractor was the very short time available for preparations: the contract for the roof structure was awarded in early December 2010 and erection had to begin as soon as 1 April 2011. So there were only four months for preparing the work and prefabrication.

Complete 3D CAD drawings of all the elements had to be ready by mid-January 2011 so that they could be made available to the cross-laminated timber supplier for precise CNC machining. To do that, the timber contractor's engineers had to design every detail and every connection so that the design team could import the results into the 3D CAD system and produce the necessary drawings for machining and assembly. The same was done for the primary structure of glued laminated timber beams and the column connections, each at a different angle.

The exact position of every panel and the erection sequence already had to be taken into account early on during the detailed design work so that the panels could be produced and delivered to site in the correct order. All CLT parts were allocated a transport number which included component designation, member number, panel thickness, and position on delivery vehicle. Structural location drawings were also prepared so that every panel could be erected in the right position on site. Some 9000 working hours were needed to produce the fabrication drawings for the timber elements, which in the end filled about 100 folders.

On site it was like assembling a giant jigsaw puzzle

Interim storage of the prefabricated timber elements was on the fabricator's premises and so storage areas on site were unnecessary. The elements were then delivered to site load by load as required and erected immediately by a crew of fifty specialists. Every day they erected between 1200 and 1500 m² of panels. A total of 160 journeys was necessary for the 8000 m³ of cross-laminated timber.

Decision in favour of a CLT roof

The tender issued by the architects included two roof decking options: OSB-sheathed timber-frame elements with integral thermal insulation and smart vapour barrier, or the cross-laminated timber version. Although the latter cost 11 per cent more, the client opted for this because it resulted in better building physics and structural results, including the more flexible arrangement of the building services inside the building.

The fact that the CLT plate is able to accommodate large wind or seismic forces and wind on the facade plus the roof cantilevers of up to 8 metres were other important arguments in favour of this option. sjf

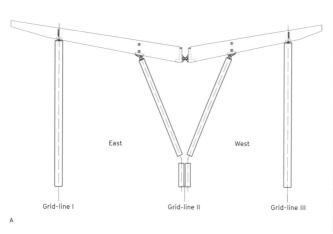

East   West

Grid-line I   Grid-line II   Grid-line III

A

B

C

D

Project **G3 Shopping Resort in Gerasdorf near Vienna**

Form of construction, shopping centre **Engineered timber structure**

Construction period, shopping centre **November 2010 to autumn 2012**

Opened to the public **Autumn 2012**

Timber structure erection, shopping centre **April to July 2011**

Financial investment **€200 million**

Gross floor area **approx. 90 000 m²**

Usable floor area **approx. 88 000 m²**

Client/developer **HY Immobilien Ypsilon GmbH, Vienna (subsidiary of BAI Bauträger Austria Immobilien GmbH, 1020 Vienna, Austria, www.bai.at)**

Project development **BAI Bauträger Austria Immobilien GmbH, 1020 Vienna, Austria, www.bai.at**

Architecture, preliminary calculations, integrated planning **ATP Architekten und Ingenieure, 1030 Vienna, Austria, www.atp.ag**

Detailed calculations, timber structure **Graf-Holztechnik GmbH, 3580 Horn, Austria, www.graf-holztechnik.at, in cooperation with Dipl.-Ing. Johann Zehetgruber Ziviltechniker GmbH, 3910 Zwettl, Austria**

Timber contractor **Graf-Holztechnik GmbH, 3580 Horn, Austria, www.graf-holztechnik.at**

Checking engineers **RWT Plus ZT GmbH, Dr.-Ing. Richard Woschitz, 1010 Vienna, Austria, www.rwt.at**

Site management **Leyrer + Graf Baugesellschaft m.b.H., 3580 Horn, Austria, www.leyrer-graf.at**

Production & supply of CLT panels: **Mayr-Melnhof Holz Reuthe GmbH, 6870 Reuthe, Austria, www.mm-holz.com, and Stora Enso Wood Products GmbH, 9462 Bad St. Leonhard, Austria, www.clt.info**

Quantity of timber used **11 500 m³**

Carbon (C) content **2875 t**

Sequestered CO_2 **10 534 t**

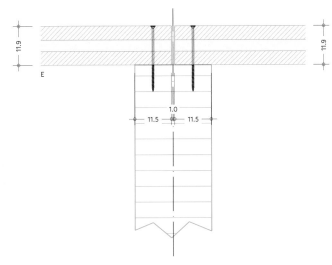

E

OSB 25 mm   Nailing to drg. 50_559_316

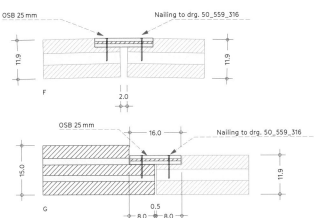

11.9   11.9

F   2.0

OSB 25 mm   16.0   Nailing to drg. 50_559_316

15.0   11.9

G   0.5
   8.0   8.0

41

H

I

J

A → Section through roof in long end sections; all supports are pinned.

B → Connection between symmetrical, inward-sloping glulam beams in the long 'roof gussets' beyond the elongated teardrop-shaped openings

C → Steel dowels and plates with elongated holes let into the timber connect the three-part glulam beams rigidly together in the middle of the roof.

D → The difference in height in the middle of the curving roof form is about 8 metres.

E → Transverse joint between CLT panels over glulam beam

F → Cross-laminated timber longitudinal joint without change in thickness

G → Cross-laminated timber longitudinal joint with change in thickness

H → Every CLT panel spans two bays. They are screwed to the glulam beams at the transverse joints.

I → Each CLT panel was erected offset by half a panel length.

J → The rebates along the edges of the panels accommodate the OSB strips.

Solid timber instead of trusses

A timber wholesaler has used the new buildings of a branch depot to demonstrate the options that modern engineered timber construction can offer. For economic reasons, solid timber beams have been used instead of open trusses for the extremely complex roof structure to the warehouse. The regular spacing of the beams results in a calm, homogeneous appearance.

Even from a distance, the huge warehouse for the Philippsburg-Huttenheim branch of timber wholesaler Scheiffele-Schmiederer (SCS) is a real eye-catcher, due to its size, on the one hand, and to its unusual roofscape, on the other. Some 3000 m³ of material are stored here, ranging from structural timber products, e.g. glued laminated timber and solid structural timber sections, right up to wood-based products such as OSB, three- and multi-ply cross-laminated timber and panels for roofs and walls. Several articulated vehicles and large commercial vehicles are available for deliveries to customers. The large quantities of stored materials and the vehicle movements had to be considered in the planning.

Less is more
Essentially, the designers chose the materials based on function and minimum costs; the aesthetics of the new building should come about through successful forms and the skilful combination of building materials. Therefore, simple industrial materials such as concrete, glued

laminated timber, steel sheet, and polycarbonate dominate. Contrasting with the concrete roads and hardstandings and fixed-base reinforced concrete columns, the entire roof structure is built from slender glulam beams.

The 160 metre long structure consists of two warehouse blocks totalling 70 metres in width. Each warehouse has one narrow and one wide monopitch roof, with different heights and sloping in opposite directions. Further storage space could be added in the future by continuing this modular principle.

Client's stipulation: no trusses for long spans
Each warehouse block is based on three bays, which is reflected in the shape of the roof. Each wide monopitch roof spans two bays, the narrow ones just one bay. Over the storage zones the spans of the glulam beams are relatively short (12 metres), continuous over two spans below the wide roof and simply supported below the narrow roof. However, the beams above the access and loading zones are all simply supported beams spanning

View of loading zone. The glulam beams carrying the monopitch roof span 24 metres from column to column, or from the longitudinal beam on the right to a post supported on the longitudinal beam on the left. The regular spacing of the glulam beams disguises the complex structural system and ensures a calm appearance.

A → Site layout showing positions of columns. The areas of the monopitch roofs coincide with the column grid.

B → Section through warehouse

C → The impressive thing about the warehouse is its size and its vigorous roofscape, which ensures an agreeable lightness.

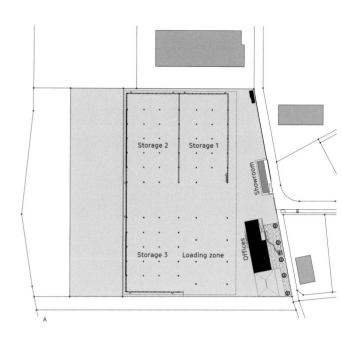

Storage 2 Storage 1

Showroom

Storage 3 Loading zone

Offices

A

Warehouse, Philippsburg

44

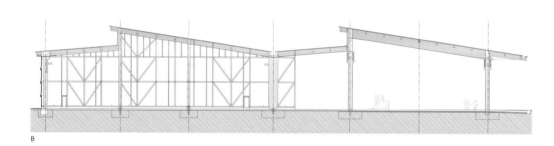

B

C

24 or 27 metres. That called for a sophisticated structural solution. For financial reasons, the client wanted the warehouse to be built of solid timber sections instead of trusses, which are complicated to assemble and erect. The designers had to devise a uniform construction configuration for the different structural situations. To do this, they specified glulam beams with approximately identical cross-sections on all main longitudinal grid-lines, functioning as continuous beams supported on the reinforced concrete columns. At the top of each column the support is in the form of a fork, providing lateral restraint to the beam, but the beams at the lower level are 'threaded' through a slot formed in the columns. The 12 to 24 metre long roof beams span between the reinforced concrete columns or run from the longitudinal beams to posts supported on the longitudinal beams at the lower level. Transverse beams spanning between the roof beams form the supporting structure for the roof decking and at the same time provide lateral restraint to the roof beams. On the outer longitudinal grid-line, the buckling length of the roof beams above the loading zone has been shortened by installing diagonal struts. They form a type of inclined truss that provides additional stability for the building.

The roof structure above the storage zones is designed according to the same principle but modified to suit the structural circumstances. Rows of K-bracing brace the roof structure.

Compartmentation for fire protection
The load-bearing structure has an F30 fire resistance rating. For fire protection purposes, the 13000 m² warehouse area is divided into fire compartments. Every storage zone forms a separate fire compartment and there is a reinforced concrete fire wall between the two rear storage zones. At the front of the building, the very wide access zone is deemed to be a separating element, and the loading zone was classed as having virtually no fire load.

Polycarbonate and metal trapezoidal profile sheets for external skin
The external walls and the roof surfaces are made from metal trapezoidal profile sheets and transparent polycarbonate sheets. The sides of the building are left open around the access and loading zones. So full weather protection is only provided for those areas where the timber is stored.

Good cross-ventilation is ensured by the rooflights and the metal trapezoidal profile sheets on the facade which are 'bent outwards' with timber fillets. The ventilation area corresponds to 2 per cent of the plan area of the building and hence the exact area required for

smoke vents. In the event of a fire, a further 3 per cent is supplied by the polycarbonate sheets in the roof; exposed to fire, they melt and drop to the floor (but produce no hazardous burning droplets).

The bent metal trapezoidal profile sheets on the facade help to reduce the bulk of this voluminous structure, giving it an elegant appearance. Transparent vertical joints in the facade help to diminish the apparent width of the building. The bottommost row of dark sheets looks like a plinth and creates the illusion of a base.

Timber box on reinforced concrete
The architects placed a two-storey office building next to the warehouse, and the quality of the former's architecture is in no way inferior to that of the latter. The roughly 34 metre long, 13.50 metre wide building rests on a roughly one metre high reinforced concrete plinth. Raising the building in this way ensures that staff in the ground-floor offices do not have to look at the tyres and chassis of the vehicles passing by, and instead are more or less on the level of the drivers. However, at the back of the building the storeroom and workshop are positioned level with the ground, i.e. not raised on a plinth.

The upper floor contains the archives and staff welfare amenities, including rooms for changing and washing, plus two long loggias. The client wanted maximum sound insulation between the two storeys and at the same time an open-plan office without any intervening columns to the right of the long access ramp. A suitable floor structure was required to span this area measuring about 10 × 10 metres and at the same time provide the necessary sound insulation. Good room acoustics were also required.

Hybrid timber and reinforced concrete construction
Apart from the plinth and the rear part of the building, which is made of precast concrete components, the office building is a timber structure. Together with the structural engineers, the architects selected the optimum design configuration for the load-bearing structure in each case depending on the logistical and architectural requirements as well as the structural and building physics needs. Therefore, the timber part of the building is a 'hybrid structure' made of very diverse timber elements. Whereas the timber construction for the walls to the ground and upper floors could be restricted to cross-laminated timber (CLT) panels and a load-bearing post-and-rail arrangement in laminated veneer lumber (LVL) around the glass facade (partly supported on timber spandrel panels), it was necessary to combine various timber elements and design approaches for the suspended floor and the roof. One

interesting detail is the lift shaft in cross-laminated timber.

The architects chose a construction consisting of timber box elements for the suspended floor over the open-plan office. Despite their low self-weight and low structural depth, these elements have a high load-carrying capacity and can span up to 8 metres. However, as the span over the open-plan office is 10 metres, the structural engineers decided to use two layers of these box elements bonded with adhesive. The suspended floor is therefore 44 centimetres deep. To improve the room acoustics, perforated boards and absorbent fleece were attached to the soffit.

And to reduce sound transmissions between the storeys, the timber boxes were filled with calcium silicate bricks and chippings. These attenuate oscillations and therefore minimise the propagation of footstep noise. Combined with the floor finishes, they help to achieve an impact sound insulation value of forty-two decibels.

Timber box elements with acoustic perforations and sound attenuation have also been used above the reception. However, the shorter span here (6.40 m) required only one layer. A floor of cross-laminated timber was adequate for all the other offices, reinforced concrete for the storeroom and workshop.

Roof as cold deck with air space and hangers for loggia
The roof structure uses 39 centimetre deep, thermally insulated hollow box elements made of FJI beams (Kerto LVL flanges + OSB webs, clad both sides). On top of those there is a secondary waterproofing layer and then an air space. As with a conventional roof frame, a purlins/rafters arrangement supports a shallow-pitch roof covered with waterproof sheeting without a

granular finish. Six 62.5 centimetre deep LVL beams were built into the roof over the length of the loggia, which cantilevers over the entrance area and ramp, so that the loggia could be suspended from glulam hangers. Each beam has a 10 metre long simply supported span and a 3.5 metre cantilever. The dead load of the roof structure, which is attached to the hollow box elements, is sufficient to balance the load on the cantilever, which means that no uplift forces act at the far end of the beam.

Passive house-compliant building envelope
The quality of the building envelope corresponds to that of a passive house. The CLT external walls to the ground and upper floors have 30 centimetres of thermal insulation between the FJI beams forming the frame. Diffusion-permeable wood fibre boards are used for the inside face to the walls. The space between the fair-face concrete facing leaf and the plinth, or the CLT spandrel panels to the open-plan office, has also been filled with 30 centimetres of thermal insulation. Well-insulated roof elements and triple-glazed windows complete the passive house-compliant building envelope. For example, the U-value of the external walls on the upper floor is 0.116 W/m²K, that of the roof 0.1004 W/m²K.

Worthy of a prize
Although the office building and the warehouse are separate and based on different design vocabularies, they nevertheless form a convincing whole. The office building was one of the first winners of the 'HolzbauPlus' competition organised by Germany's Federal Ministry of Food & Agriculture for the first time in 2013. It was selected as a winner in the 'Commercial Buildings' category out of 150 submissions. sjf

A

B

C

A → Reinforced concrete columns with slots for 'threading' the lower longitudinal beams and fork supports at the top for the roof beams

B → The LIGNATUR flat elements (LFE) were assembled with the help of steel beams matching the depth of the elements, which provided supports for the suspended floor.

C → After erection, the elements are filled with chippings and calcium silicate bricks are laid in the slots in the top of each suspended floor element to act as sound attenuators.

D → The soffits to the floor elements are perforated to improve the room acoustics and have one major advantage: structural carcass = fitting-out.

E → The new office building is a compact block allowing many views in and out. The facade is divided into two zones: a 'mineral' one below, an 'organic' one in wood above.

F → Exploded view: apart from the plinth made of precast concrete elements at the back of the building, this is a timber building with a passive house-compliant envelope; it undercuts Germany's 2009 energy conservation legislation by 40 per cent.

D

E

Project New warehouse and office building for Scheiffele-Schmiederer KG in Philippsburg-Huttenheim

Form of construction Engineered timber construction

Completed 2011

Construction period Warehouse: February to October 2011; offices: April 2011 to February 2012

Costs not specified

Usable floor area 11 335 m² (warehouse), 767 m² (offices)

Enclosed volume 142 500 m³ (warehouse), 4437 m³ (offices)

Client Scheiffele-Schmiederer KG, 76661 Philippsburg, Germany, www.scheiffele-schmiederer.de

Architecture gumpp . heigl . schmitt architekten, 80336 Munich, Germany, www.gumpp-heigl-schmitt.de

Structural engineering Warehouse: Dr Linse Ingenieure GmbH, 80333 Munich, Germany, www.drlinse.de; offices: Ingenieurbüro von Fragstein, 76829 Landau, Germany, www.von-fragstein.com

Timber contractor Warehouse: Hess Timber GmbH & Co. KG, 63924 Kleinheubach, Germany, www.hess-timber.com; offices: Holzbau Tretter, 67435 Neustadt/Weinstraße-Mußbach, Germany, www.mit-gunst-und-verlaub.mussbach.de

Checking engineers Warehouse & offices: Ing.-Büro Blaß & Eberhard, 76227 Karlsruhe, Germany, www.ing-bue.de

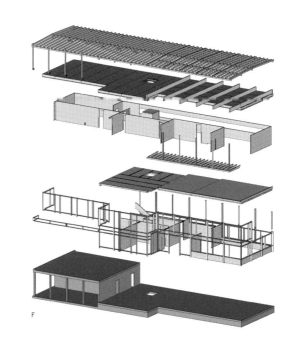

F

New heart in an old line

Since 2013 lower Austria has had a new landmark: the new operations centre at Laubenbachmühle station on the Mariazell Railway. A design with a timber roof structure triumphed in the architectural competition. The ribbed shell spans all the different parts of the station but still allows ample daylight into the interior.

Some years ago, Austrian Federal Railways announced its plan to close all unprofitable branch lines. The state of Lower Austria reacted to this by taking over a number of the lines, including the Mariazell Railway, and keeping them running for tourists.

This line has become the star representing all branch lines. It was built in the early 19th century and was the first narrow gauge line to be electrified. Starting in St Pölten, it runs into the Pielach Valley and then over the mountains to Mariazell.

As the route is unique also in terms of its cultural history, the state decided to upgrade the line and equip it with new rolling stock. However, the old workshops and facilities in St Pölten were already more like a museum and so a new operations centre for the technical infra-structure had to be built as well.

A tourist attraction like Switzerland's Glacier Express

Laubenbachmühle station was chosen as the ideal location for the new operations centre. Ideal because not only is it in the middle of the line, it is also the place where the breathtaking trip to Mariazell begins, where the train winds its way up the mountain in wide loops. The declared aim was to create a tourist attraction modelled on the Glacier Express in Switzerland.

Competition produces the perfect answer

An open, international competition for the master planning and implementation of this demanding project was initiated in 2011. The specification covered the construction of three buildings: a shed for storing the rolling stock, a workshop, and a roof over the station. Besides the operational functions, the complete ensemble also had to take tourism into account.

United compactly under one roof and well integrated into the landscape

The winning design brought together all three buildings under one roof and in doing so created a homogeneous structure that blends into its surroundings. The jury also liked the idea of using timber for the structure as Lower Austria favours ecological forms of construction.

Furthermore, the architects positioned the workshop and the rolling stock shed one behind the other – instead of next to each other as is common for railway facilities – yet were still able to combine them skilfully with the through-station. Workshop and shed are positioned a short distance apart alongside the valley line, turned at a small angle to the line itself. The ensuing 'gap' between the buildings at the apex of this broad V shape created a spacious entrance forecourt that steers visitors towards the platforms.

Interior view of the storage shed with its five tracks. The resolved roof structure and the special wall structures composed of steel columns and timber-clad timber-frame walls allow plenty of glass to be included to admit ample daylight and provide all-round views in and out.

The diamond-shaped framing to the shallow barrel vault roofs is intended to simulate criss-crossing tracks. The form of the long, undulating lines of the vegetation on the surrounding hills was taken up by the architects for the design of the curving roof. In the process they also succeeded in integrating the buildings in such a way that their height is hardly apparent.

Form follows function

Both shed and workshop measure approximately 64 metres long × 37.5 metres wide – dimensions specified right from the start to suit train lengths and track numbers. Inside the shed, five trains can be stored alongside each other. Directly adjacent are ancillary facilities and a sixth track for the washing shed. The workshop building has three tracks and includes various rooms for storage, working, plant, and staff, including changing and sanitary facilities.

The 12 metre maximum building height and the radii of the curving barrel vault roof with its rising end section were dictated by the headroom required by the trains and the minimum clearances between train, overhead lines, and roof or workshop facilities.

Diamond pattern formed by primary beams and diagonal secondary beams

The two identical sheds each have four longitudinal grid-lines (A, B, B', and C) about 11 metres apart. Three of these form the support lines for the roof structure, i.e. a ribbed reinforced concrete wall designed by the structural engineers as the end support on grid-line A, reinforced concrete deep beams on columns on grid-line B as the intermediate support, and pairs of steel columns with intervening timber-clad timber-frame walls as the other end support on grid-line C.

The roughly 36 metre long glued laminated timber main beams (b × h = 24 cm × 110 – 150 – 123 cm, GL32) of the roof structure form shallow arches spanning the three grid-lines at a spacing of 5 metres; the first bay (A–B) measures almost 11 metres, the second (B–C) about 22 metres.

Whereas at their end supports these main beams have pinned connections (at one end raking columns projecting from the ribbed reinforced concrete wall, at the other the pairs of steel columns), in the middle they pass through deep cut-outs in the top of the deep beam forming the intermediate support, which thus constitutes a type of fork support.

Intersecting diagonally with the main beams at an angle of about 25 degrees are the roughly 12 metre long glued laminated timber secondary beams – likewise shallow arches with varying depths (b × h = 22 × 150 – 123 cm / 138 – 150 cm / 110 – 138 cm, GL24). Each one therefore spans an 11 metre longitudinal bay between grid-lines.

The primary and secondary roof beams thus always intersect at the supports or 'cross' in the middle of the large bay. This produced a triangular or diamond-type grid in which the architects have placed the rooflights.

The structural engineers developed the nodes together with the timber contractor. Special steel plates were fitted to the secondary beams (intersecting at an acute angle), which were then connected with one bolt on site. This solution enabled simple, fast erection and rendered the connections almost invisible. A highly accurate 3D CAD model was used to transfer the design data to the machinery for CNC fabrication.

Space for services between roof structure and roof decking

The fire protection concept included a sprinkler installation for the entire complex. In order to provide room for the sprinkler pipework and other services, a continuous space was provided between the roof structure and the roof decking by raising the decking on battens at the same level as the ribs of the roof elements. At the same time these function as the supporting framework for the soffit. This solution essentially ruled out using the roof decking as a stiffening diaphragm, which would have been very awkward anyway with such a large number of rooflights.

Structural stability

Lateral support to prevent buckling of the main beams is provided at a spacing of about 11 metres – via the fork supports at the reinforced concrete deep beam and via torsion-resistant connections to the beams over the platforms.

Near the end supports, above the high-level windows in the external walls, lateral stability for the beams is ensured by bolting them to the roof elements, in some cases combined with steel X-bracing. Furthermore, in the 22 metre shed span there are strengthened ribs in the roof decking which are designed as continuous members capable of taking tension or compression and form 'local roof diaphragms' in the 5 metre wide gable end span. These members transfer the bracing forces to the reinforced concrete wall, or rather the bracing point in the outer wall.

A-frames in timber-frame walls as 'surrogate columns'

The timber-frame walls suspended between the steel columns on steel brackets were supplied as prefabricated elements measuring 4 metres high × 10 metres long. Each element consists of substantial top and bottom chords plus a sort of A-frame with one vertical post. They are insulated and clad both sides. The frame is located in the middle of the element, and as there is only one steel column

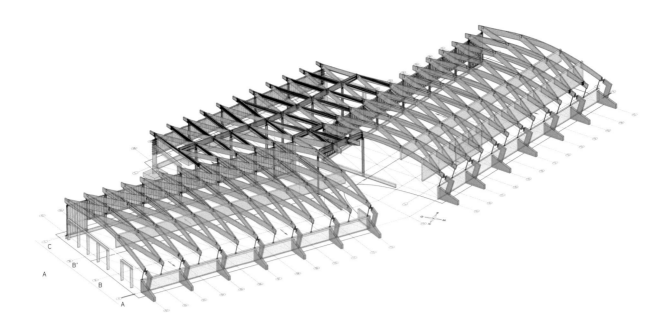

B

C

A → Isometric view of the roof structure; the workshop (left) and rolling stock shed (right) are identical structures. The primary beams (turquoise) every 5 metres span two bays, the shorter secondary beams (olive green) intersect with these at an angle.

B → Resembling a giant funnel, the entrance forecourt between the workshop and the rolling stock shed channels visitors towards the platforms. The glass facades permit visitors to see into the buildings left and right.

C → Workshop and rolling stock shed in a line alongside the tracks. The station itself links them skilfully to form a homogeneous complex that blends into the landscape.

A → Space for services (sprinkler pipework and electric cables) was included between roof structure and underside of roof decking.

B → Interior view of workshop building with overhead crane

C → The parallel main beams span two bays. The shorter secondary beams are mounted diagonally between these. Main and secondary beams are connected above the middle of the large bay with just one bolt.

D → View of gable end of workshop building. Each main beam varies in depth and has pinned connections at the end supports. The intermediate support is a fork.

E → Simply supported beams span the approximately 55 metre long × 20–25 metre wide station. A beam of the same depth supported on pairs of steel columns forms the intermediate support.

F → Entrance to Laubenbachmühle station seen from inside

52

B

C

D

A

E

every 10 metres, it carries the loads from a main beam (which are every 5 metres) and acts as a 'surrogate column' transferring the loads to the steel columns on either side.

Simply supported beams for roof over station
Grid-line C marks the transition between shed or workshop and the station roof, whose load-bearing structure is designed to the same principles as those of the other roofs. In this case though, the intermediate support is a beam of the same depth which is supported on pairs of steel columns. The primary and secondary roof beams are connected here in such a way that they act as simply supported beams.

Transparency for a distance of 3 metres above the ground is assured here by using pairs of steel columns combined with 10 metre wide, timber-clad timber-frame walls. These form the external wall and enable passengers to watch trains on the track beyond the building.

Roof elements for thermal/sound insulation and moisture control
All roof elements contain thermal insulation and have a smart vapour barrier – apart from those above the washing shed, which include a vapour-tight foil that prevents moisture infiltrating the construction.

Perforated cross-laminated timber has been used for the soffit to each roof element – again with the exception of the washing shed. These boards satisfy the reverberation time requirements for the various interior areas.

Laubenbachmühle as the focus for travel and culture
More or less exactly thirteen months after announcing the result of the competition, the first train was rolling on the newly laid track – a construction period certainly worthy of a prize itself! The new operations centre has been included in the Lower Austria Exhibition 2015 and therefore this innovative building will be in the public eye. sjf

Project Laubenbachmühle station and railway operations centre on the Mariazell Railway in Frankenfels, Austria

Form of construction Engineered timber structure

Completed 2013

Construction period December 2011 to May 2013

Costs €20 million (net)

Client NÖVOG Niederösterreichische Verkehrsorganisationsgesellschaft m.b.H., 3100 St Pölten, Austria, www.noevog.at

Architecture / Master plan Architekt Zieser Ziviltechniker GmbH, 3100 St Pölten, and 1010 Vienna, Austria, www.zieserarchitekt.com

Structural engineering, timber, structural details RWT plus ZT GmbH, Dipl.-Ing. Dr Richard Woschitz; project manager: Ing. Anton Oster MSc, 1010 Vienna, Austria, www.rwt.at

Timber contractor Rubner Holzbau GmbH, 3200 Ober-Grafendorf, Austria, www.rubner.com

Quantity of timber used 1250 m³

Carbon (C) content 312.5 t

Sequestered CO_2 1146 t

F

A new approach to timber-frame construction

An airtight, non-glued, solid timber fair-face board has been used for the first time in the construction of an organic supermarket in Luxembourg. This invention from the Black Forest opens up extensive options for timber construction.

Agricultural operations around Windhof in Luxembourg have been organised according to organic principles since 1988. The investment of the organic farmers has not stopped at modernising their farms. Indeed, it has included the construction of their own supermarket for organic produce. Organised in the form of a large-scale farm shop with a sales area of about 380 m², a full range of products is on offer, first and foremost the products of BIOG, the Luxembourg organic farmers cooperative. One fundamental idea behind this location is to re-acquaint customers with the idea of foodstuffs produced in their region. For example, windows around the sales area enable customers to see into the neighbouring stalls. Opened in February 2014, the organic supermarket uses a new type of ecological timber-frame construction. This aspect was important for the client collective because the aim was – in line with the philosophy of their organic farms – to achieve a building without health or pollution issues.

The building biology alternative to OSB and particleboard

Conventional timber-frame buildings are stiffened with OSB and/or particleboard sheathing, which can contain dangerous isocyanates or formaldehyde. However, the load-bearing timber frame of the organic supermarket is clad and stabilised by a non-glued solid timber board that has been on the market since 2013. The new board was invented by Dieter Junker, who christened his building biology alternative GFM (= Glue-Free Massive). This innovative product contains no building chemicals

whatsoever, consists entirely of pure Black Forest softwood that is only sawn, planed, and dried. The crux of the invention is that the individual pieces of timber are joined by purely mechanical means using a centuries-old, traditional carpentry joint – the dovetail, which in addition to providing horizontal stability, can also be loaded in tension to a certain extent. The planks making up this solid timber product, with a standard thickness of 30 millimetres, are laid diagonally, which means that the structural forces involved in bracing a timber-frame building can be resisted more effectively. The structural analysis is carried out according to Eurocode 5 as sheathing with diagonal bracing. The production of the GFM panels is based on five individual planks of indigenous, PEFC-certified silver fir or spruce with a residual moisture content of about 12 per cent into which traditional carpentry dovetail joints are machined. Afterwards, the planks are pressed together under high pressure to form panels 3.21 or 3.91 metres long and 62 centimetres wide. Finally, a laser scans the solid timber surface to detect any knot holes or flaws, which are then sealed with a totally innocuous hot wax. The panel is then airtight as a whole, as testing and approval to DIN 13829 has confirmed. Air permeabilities between q50 0.01 and 0.23 m³/m²h have been achieved in different installation situations.

Client's request: facing quality

The GFM panels do not require a separate vapour barrier. Two carpenters can install the panels with the help of a mechanical suspension system. The panels have an

The interplay of vertical and horizontal external cladding lends the organic supermarket a dynamic factor.

overlapping joint that can be fitted with a waterproofing tape to achieve a certain airtightness where this is important. By using purely timber for stability and achieving airtightness without sheeting or foil, timber-frame construction can now make inroads into the market for ecological and non-polluting forms of construction, which up until now have been the province of solid timber construction.

It is due to this Luxembourg client collective that the Junker company has added a sanded, fair-face version to its range of GFM products. While considering the GFM panel, the farmers had the idea of leaving the wooden surface exposed inside the supermarket and not covering it with, for example, plasterboard, as is usually the case. Although Junker viewed this request with scepticism because of the dimensional tolerances of the individual planks and pointed out that the invention was only intended to be a substitute for OSB, the wooden surfaces have remained visible. This concept of a simple technical product that stabilises the timber frame but also satisfies building biology and visual demands has convinced all those involved with the project. By omitting the plasterboard, and the time-consuming skimming of the joints associated with that, it was possible to brace the timber frame with the GFM panels for the same price as cheaper, conventional systems. A coat of oil on the sanded wooden surfaces was the only finishing needed. Apart from sheathing to timber-frame walls, the solid GFM panels can also be used for floors, roofs, and facades.

Luxembourg longhouse tradition
When designing the organic supermarket with its elongated rectangular form, architect Stephan Hain let himself be inspired by the Luxembourg longhouse tradition on which the old part of the farmyard is based. In order to combine the old, mineral form with the new, wooden one, Hain featured parts of an old rubble stone wall – demolished to make way for the supermarket – in the entrance area. His design for the foundations and ground floor was both simple and efficient. A layer of cellular glass granulate to prevent rising damp is covered by a floor slab of industry-grade concrete which contains the underfloor heating system. Cellular glass is made entirely from foamed scrap glass and is primarily used for thermal insulation and stabilisation tasks. As this relatively lightweight material is incompressible, watertight, non-toxic, load-bearing, and virtually rot-proof, no expensive layers were needed below the ground floor slab as is usually the case when insulation is laid in direct contact with the ground. The surface of the concrete ground slab was polished after initial drying and so the floor was ready immediately after completing the structural carcass. The high cost of laying additional

insulating, sealing, heating, or other layers could therefore be saved.

Cellulose insulation and green roof
Inside the building the solid timber panels were left exposed. Outside, however, they were clad with silver fir battens. In order to integrate the historical and architectural context, Hain used a grey colour to differentiate the area around the demolished rubble stone wall and therefore bonded it to the neighbouring old rubble stone farmyard buildings. The rhombus-shaped battens forming the cladding on the supermarket are vertical on many walls. Only on the link to the store and the house are they horizontal. In addition, the timber battens were treated with a special building biology-compliant softwood lye so that they achieve an even grey colour as quickly as possible. The roof, conceived as a timber joist structure, includes factory-produced spaces that are finished with veneer plywood boards on the underside and wood cement particleboard on top. As with the load-bearing external walls, these spaces were also filled with blown cellulose insulation. On top of that there is a 12 centimetre air space closed off with tongue and groove boards, then PVC-free waterproofing on which the green roof is laid with a 40 centimetre deep substrate. In order to guarantee that the cavity beneath the green roof really works as a ventilation void, fresh air from the supermarket's ventilation system is drawn into the air space within the roof. A bypass arrangement prevents condensation in the air space due to high humidity in the summer. Sensors at exposed positions measure humidity and temperature constantly and therefore prevent dampness in the roof.

Thermoactive floor slab uses waste heat
The energy supply concept involves several stages. For example, the supermarket has underfloor heating based on a thermoactive floor slab concept. The heating pipes were cast directly into the ground floor slab. The concrete slab is fed with waste heat from the refrigeration system for the foodstuffs, i.e. directly from the freezers. A heat exchanger extracts the heat from the condenser and feeds this to an interim storage unit. This reaches a temperature adequate for heating the supermarket, as a room temperature of only 19°C is sufficient all year round and the energy distribution over the total floor area requires only a low flow temperature of just over 30°C. Radiators are only installed in the offices and changing rooms to cope with the lowest temperatures in winter. There is also a hot-air curtain at the entrance which is fed from the house's central heating system.

While constructing the supermarket, the client collective took the opportunity to renew the heating

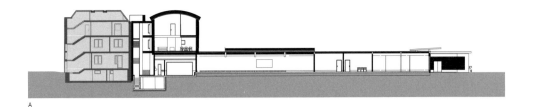

A

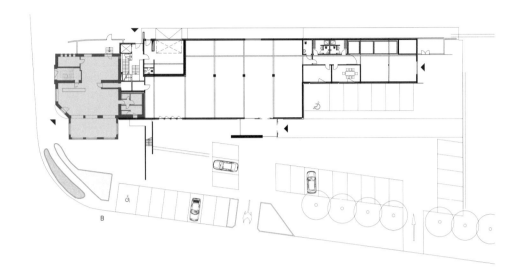

B

C

A + B → The long, rectangular alignment and the plan form of the supermarket (ground floor shown here) draw their inspiration from Luxembourg longhouse tradition.

C → Natural materials and healthy foodstuffs – organic agriculture and ecological timber construction fused together in Luxembourg longhouse architecture.

B

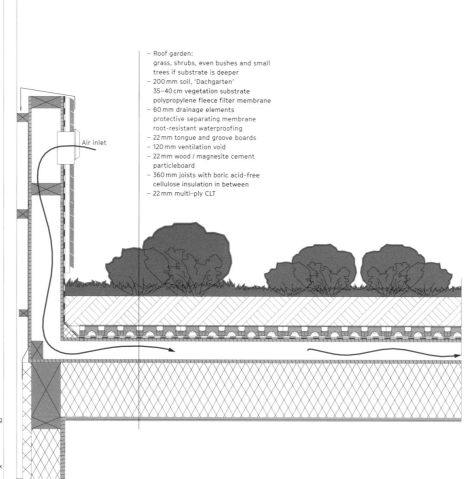

Screen at top of wall: 60 × 90 mm battens
projecting above parapet

Air inlet

– Roof garden:
  grass, shrubs, even bushes and small
  trees if substrate is deeper
– 200 mm soil, 'Dachgarten'
  35–40 cm vegetation substrate
  polypropylene fleece filter membrane
– 60 mm drainage elements
  protective separating membrane
  root-resistant waterproofing
– 22 mm tongue and groove boards
– 120 mm ventilation void
– 22 mm wood / magnesite cement
  particleboard
– 360 mm joists with boric acid-free
  cellulose insulation in between
– 22 mm multi-ply CLT

– 60 mm vertical timber sheathing
  (60 × 60 mm, 60 × 90 mm)
– 40 mm horizontal battens
  (40 × 60 mm)
– 60 mm wood fibre insulating
  board, treated with paraffin wax
– 200 mm timber studs with boric
  acid-free cellulose insulation in
  between
– 30 mm GFM diagonal sheathing

A

system in the existing building as well. A solar thermal system was installed on the roof of the store, the heat gains of which can be backed up with a pellet-fired boiler as required. The old gas-fired boiler is now used as a backup system or for coping with peak loads. mwl

C

A → The ventilation for the green roof is integrated into the central ventilation system. Fresh air from outside is first used to ventilate the roof structure before it is fed into the supermarket.

B → Initially, the solid timber panels were only intended as a building biology-compliant bracing alternative for the timber-frame walls. Only later did the idea of leaving these exposed come about.

C → The diagonal arrangement of the solid timber panels not only improves their structural function, but also creates a pleasant interior.

Architecture hainarchitektur, 6632 Wasserbillig, Luxembourg, www.hainarchitektur.lu

Client Demeter Hof Guy and Sylvie Meyers-Weis, Windhof, Luxembourg, www.naturata.lu

Timber contractor Holzbau Henz GmbH, 54311 Trierweiler, Germany, www.holzbauhenz.de

Floor area 557 m²

of which sales area 377 m²

Heating requirement 64 kWh/m²a (=thermal performance rating C)

Primary energy requirement 28 kWh/m²a (=total energy efficiency rating A) (Note: waste heat from cooling must not be included)

Airtightness 1.18 1/h

Costs €1 million

Quantity of timber used 248 m³

Carbon (C) content 62 t

Sequestered CO_2 227 t

Healthy living and working

A mixed commercial/ residential building that is made of prefabricated solid timber elements and takes into account build- ing biology aspects has been built in South Tyrol. The certified energy-plus building has a zero-emis- sions energy supply and uses no sheeting, foil, or automatic ventilation.

Timber contractor Casa Salute S.r.l. has relocated its main office in South Tyrol from Bozen to the Schwemm Business Park in Margreid. For the client it was important that the two-storey timber building, which also serves as a home, be built using ecological and climate-neutral materials and systems. The design had to take account of the narrow, elongated shape of the plot. Therefore, the architect, Marco Sette, designed a south-facing timber building with a quadruple-glazed curving panorama front facade to link the broad lowland valley with the interior and achieve maximum solar gains. The plan form of this two-storey mixed commercial/residential building resembles a right-angled triangle with an outward-curving hypotenuse. The curved glazed facade supplies the ground-floor office and showroom area with ample day- light until late in the day in the summer and also achieves significant solar gains in the winter.

Although there are fewer windows in the living quarters upstairs, the area of glass is still generous and provides views over the surrounding fields and vine- yards. On this level there is also a spacious terrace that extends from the main building across to the flat roof of the guest chalet. This chalet has been included to give customers the opportunity to experience personally the healthy interior climate of a solid timber building. An elliptical staircase with a polygonal wall made

of separate, gently curved solid timber elements forms the heart of the two-storey timber building. Framed by load-bearing timber columns, it connects the two floors. Marco Sette took this as his starting point for the entire interior layout.

Building based on solid timber elements
The Rombach-Nur-Holz system has been used for the building. This system is based on fully prefabricated solid wall, floor, and roof elements that can be quickly as- sembled with the help of a crane to provide a structural carcass. The system elements consist of layers of soft- wood planks (fir and spruce) in various thicknesses with a cross-banded lay-up and joined with hardwood screws to form compact, solid timber components. For structural reasons, the timber engineers have included an addi- tional complete layer of timber sections 6 to 8 centimetres deep plus a layer of planks attached at an angle of 45 degrees to guarantee the strength permanently. The use of hardwood screws made from beech renders adhesives, metal fasteners, and metal dowels superfluous and maintains the single-material 'just wood' concept of the whole system.

Assembling the solid timber elements involves first pressing internal threads into the layers of planks into which the beech screws are fitted. As the hardwood

The curving section of the building is a response to the particular site and allows the generously sized window areas to provide ample daylight and good solar gains.

screws have a moisture content of 6 to 8 per cent and the softwood wall elements a residual moisture content of 12 to 13 per cent, the compensatory moisture movements within the wood can be exploited as an additional stabilising factor: the drier beech screws tighten in the direction of the moister planks. The result is a stable structural connection within the solid timber element preventing settlement of the building or shrinkage cracks in the wood. In addition, the wood that is compressed by pressing the threads tries to regain its original form, which again improves the strength of the entire system. This good stability in conjunction with the low flexibility guaranteed by the solid wood screws also provides maximum safety in earthquake regions. The wave-type forces of earth tremors can be absorbed to a large extent within the wall itself before the junctions with other components are affected, which is where most damage occurs. Furthermore, the wooden screws provide greater protection than metal fasteners because they do not pull out as quickly. At junctions with other parts of the structure, tongue and groove joints planed in the facing layers prevent draughts.

Upside-down floor element

The solid timber building was conceived as diffusion-permeable to achieve an optimum interior climate in which a relative humidity between 30 and 55 per cent prevails – the healthy range considered pleasant by building occupants. The external walls to Casa Salute have been deliberately kept simple. They consist of a 26 centimetre thick solid timber element with 16 centimetre thick insulation made of ecological wood fibre insulating boards which help the wall to reach a theoretical U-value of 0.13 W/m²K. Heavy-duty anchors connect the solid timber elements to the concrete ground floor slab. The elements were levelled with the help of an 8 × 10 cm larch sole plate. On the outside the external walls are clad in weather-resistant larch or finished with a natural lime render. One clever timber architecture idea saved the client the cost of the subfloor materials and floor covering for the upper floor: a solid timber suspended floor 25 centimetres deep was installed upside-down with the facing (soffit) layer on top. Downstairs, a suspended ceiling was installed, which provided space for services and a thermoacoustic natural insulation material. In addition, this solid floor construction with its high timber content has a high specific heat capacity. The flat roof is made from 25 centimetre deep solid timber elements insulated with 20 centimetre wood fibre insulating boards which help the roof to achieve a theoretical U-value of 0.12 W/m²K.

Zero-emissions energy supply

The original idea was to install a tiled stove in the middle of the building to cover the base load for both floors. However, as emissions had to be avoided completely, this idea was abandoned, which also made the building of a chimney unnecessary. Instead, an efficient coil heating system with small polypropylene tubes (capillaries) was installed in the loam plaster to the suspended ceiling. The system works as a radiant heating system based on healthy, long-wave radiant heat and requires only 50 litres of water for 350 m² of floor area. The tiled stove was also fitted with capillary tubes. Compared with conventional coil heating systems, which use just a few pipes, this system consists of a large number of small, closely spaced, water-filled capillaries with outside diameters of 3.4 or 4.3 millimetres, which constitute a much larger surface area. Such a system can cover virtually the entire area of the surfaces used. As a result, low flow temperatures of 25 to 27°C are sufficient to create a comfortable room temperature – with significant energy-savings. Furthermore, such a system can be used for cooling in summer, too, because water with a flow temperature of about 16°C can then be pumped through the capillaries. Two separate hydraulic water circuits are used for this, separated by a stainless steel heat exchanger. Another advantage is the fact that the prefabricated capillary tube mats are very thin, so they can be laid directly below the floor covering and above the screed, for instance. The energy can therefore be supplied to the room faster and more efficiently than is the case with conventional coil heating systems, which respond comparatively sluggishly and require a long warm-up time.

Hybrid collectors and heat pumps

The capillary tube system is fed from two sources. Hybrid collectors are installed on the flat roof. These hybrid collectors contain separate solar energy systems – photovoltaic (electricity) and solar thermal (hot water) – in one panel. The electricity they produce (installed output = 5 watts, area = 33.70 m²) is used in the building itself. The hybrid collector is cooled by a heat transfer medium, which helps to keep the photovoltaic module within a range conducive to efficient electricity generation for longer – resulting in yields up to 20 per cent higher. The optimum solar cell temperature for maximum efficiency is about 25°C. The energy yield drops by about 0.33 to 0.5 per cent per degree Celsius rise in temperature, which leads to losses during the summer months, when yields should reach their maximum. At the same time, the heat extracted from the cooling system is used to heat hot water or as a backup for the space heating. When insufficient heat is available, an air/water-water/water

A

B

A → The suspended floor to this building is also in solid timber, which was quickly erected with the help of a crane.

B → A large number of small-diameter tubes distribute the energy over the entire area of the solid timber floor soffit, which is finished with loam plaster.

C → Long screws join the prefabricated solid wall elements at the corners.

D → Longitudinal section of the two-storey, energy-plus, solid timber building

C

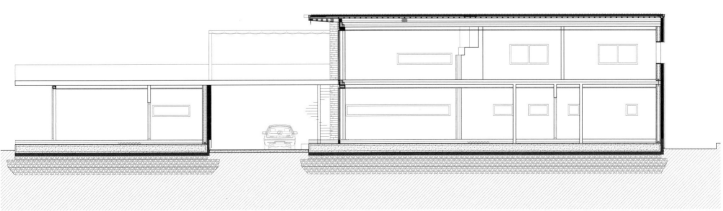

D

hybrid heat pump – powered directly by the photovoltaic panels – is activated. The source energy for the water-water module is the heated coolant water from the hybrid collectors, provided this has a suitable temperature. Afterwards, the hybrid heat pump switches over automatically to the air-water module and uses the outside air as the heat transfer medium. Two 500 litre interim storage units integrated into the system ensure that the hybrid heat pumps only work during the day with solar-powered electricity, because they provide enough energy for heating and hot water during the night. The excess is fed into the public grid. mwl

A

A → Meetings and training sessions are also held in the office area on the ground floor.

B → Plan of ground floor of mixed commercial / residential building with the showhouse in the centre

C → In terms of form and design, the solid timber building fits in with the natural line of the valley and is positioned on the narrow plot to make the best use of solar energy.

Client Casa Salute S.r.l., 39042 Margreid, Italy, www.casa-salute.it

Architecture Studio M7 – architect Marco Sette, 39100 Bozen, Italy, www.m-7.it

Timber elements Rombach Bauholz und Abbund GmbH, 77784 Oberharmersbach, Germany, www.nur-holz.com

Insulation, render & plaster Paul Pitschl company, 39040 Aldein, Italy, www.zimmerei-pitschl.it

Structural engineering Ing. Attilio Marchetti Rossi, 61121 Pesaro, Italy, www.marchettirossi.com

Glass facades Wolf Artec, 39040 Natz-Schabs, Italy, www.wolf-fenster.it

Building inspection & approval Ing. Erich Habicher, 39059 Oberbozen / Ritten, Italy

Building services consultants Energytech / Ing. Norbert Klammsteiner, 39100 Bozen, Italy, www.energytech.it

Geomantic report Georg Ungerer, 39040 Kurtatsch, Italy, www.georgungerer.it

Light switch system with piezoelectricity Opus company, 64385 Reichelsheim, Germany, www.opusgreen.net

Heating system Clina GmbH, 13435 Berlin, Germany, www.clina.de

Net floor area 350.00 m²

Transmission heat losses during heating period QT 9597 kWh/a

Ventilation heat losses during heating period QV 1578 kWh/a

Internal heat gains during heating period Qi 3936 kWh/a

Passive solar heat gains during heating period Qs 6496 kWh/a

Certificate Klimahaus Gold-Nature

Costs €900 000

Quantity of timber used 180 m³

Carbon (C) content 45 t

Sequestered CO$_2$ 165 t

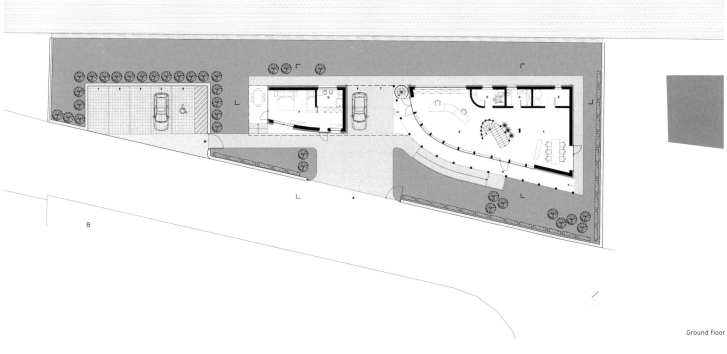

Ground floor

B

C

Sports and leisure facilities

Sports hall

Indoor rollerblade arena

Acquaworld

Les Thermes

Multifunction stadium

Simple, but effective

Since being completed in August 2012, the large sports hall serving two schools has been a real eye-catcher in Sargans. Right from the start, reducing the building to the essentials was a priority for ecological reasons. The special aesthetics, achieved with the very latest timber construction technology, is based on simple, but effective design devices and can be attributed to the early, close cooperation between the architects and the structural engineers.

The new sports hall in Sargans in St Gallen canton nestles between the high peaks of the Pizol, Falknis, and Gonzen mountains. An almost 30-year-old sports hall stood on this site before the new facility was built. Over the years it had suffered to such an extent that the cost of refurbishing it to a modern standard plus extending it to cope with increased demand – a solution that would not have been satisfactory in either constructional or operational terms – was only slightly less than that of building a new sports hall. So the client, St Gallen Building Authority, opted for demolition and a new building, and organised an anonymous, single-stage architectural competition in 2008.

Tight constraints for a great idea

The building authority placed the focus of the project on sustainability and regional value-creation. They called for the Swiss Minergie standard, keeping to a fixed budget of 20 million Swiss francs (about 16.4 million euros at the time) plus low upkeep and disposal costs. In addition, the construction period should be kept as short as possible so that sports activities would not be interrupted for too long. Another requirement was to use the existing pile foundations of the previous building for the new structure because the subsoil in this area, once a marsh of the Rhine, is very poor. With all these restrictions and stipulations, the architects' competition entry already

The design for the new sports hall had to guarantee sustainable architecture on the one hand, provide inspiration on the other. These two factors should guarantee long-term acceptance among local residents.

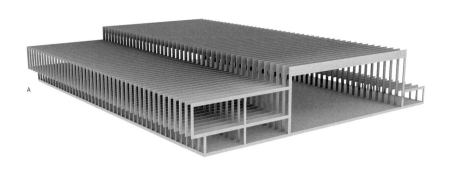

A

D

E

B

F

G

C

A → 3D computer graphic of loadbearing structure; left: changing rooms, sanitary facilities, and equipment storage; centre: playing area; right: equipment storage.

B → The slender frame members ensure that users have an almost uninterrupted view of the outside world and also allow plenty of daylight into the building.

C → The close spacing of the frames gives the interior its character; the load-bearing structure functions as a design element.

D → With frame members only 14 centimetres wide, temporary scaffolding was required when assembling the members prior to erection. After that they could be lifted into position with a crane.

E → Frame beams with their pre-installed GSA connectors after delivery to the building site

F → The GSA fasteners are fitted in the frame corners and are hardly noticeable after erection.

G → Double-T elements with closed soffits were fitted between the frame beams to form a roof plate.

H → The 7 metre high glass facade on the north-east side has no diagonal bracing and so ensures good, even daylighting inside the building.

I → Plan of ground floor

J → Section

71

H

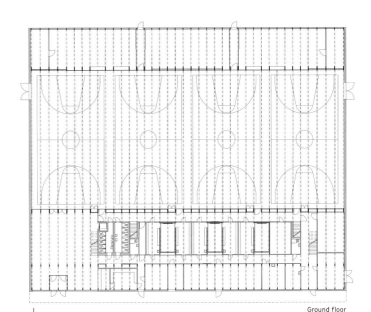

I

Ground floor

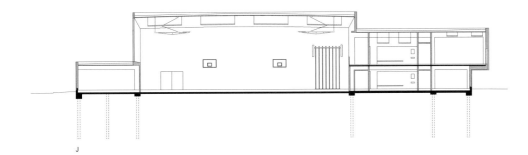

J

conceived the sports hall as a lightweight timber structure – which turned out to be the criterion that made their design the winner.

The design idea and aim of the planning team was to create a sensuous, expressive, premium structural carcass with a load-bearing structure of high-quality timber used sensibly and without depleting resources. To optimise costs and the use of resources, the architects therefore checked whether operations or materials could be saved or components omitted at every stage of the project. This careful, consequential architecture is now the trademark of the roughly 66 metre long, 56 metre wide structure.

In terms of urban planning, the new sports hall fits in with the neighbouring school, already refurbished and extended, and its position within the campus. One way in which the new 10 metre high sports hall manages the transition between the large volume of the building and the smaller buildings of the surroundings is that there is a lower, single-storey wing along the north-east, longitudinal side of the hall. Equipment is stored in this wing. Inside the sports hall itself, double-layer synthetic leather curtains can be lowered to divide the interior into two, three or four smaller areas as required. In the two-storey section, which is on the other, south-west, side of the building there are fitness and gymnastics rooms on the upper floor, a kitchen, plant room and storerooms for outdoor equipment on the ground floor, and cloakrooms and sanitary facilities on both floors. The internal layout is therefore simple and pragmatic, with ceiling heights chosen to suit the usage requirements.

Sensuous presence thanks to new methods

Forty slender glued laminated timber frames made of indigenous spruce in various strength grades constitute the primary structure to the almost 30 metre wide sports hall. As the forces acting on the structure are not the same at all points and, consequently, the same glulam strengths are not required everywhere, the grades could be adapted to save costs. Closely spaced at 1.65 metres, these frames look like a delicate wall, or ceiling, of timber slats.

In the sports hall the architects positioned the suspended overhead light fittings between the frames. When in use in the evenings, the lights contrast nicely with the black soffit elements, which are also designed to improve the room acoustics. Together with the beams, they create a visually appealing play of light and colour that is reflected in the continuous, 7 metre high glass front to the sports hall. It needed engineering tricks to keep the glazing free from bracing so daylight can enter through the windows and spread out evenly over the entire playing area. The closely spaced load-bearing

structure of slender cross-sections continues through all parts of the building and hence leads to convincing logic and exceptional aesthetics. This 'social sustainability' was just as important to the architects as the ecological aspects. For even if the 2500 m³ of untreated timber used here correspond to an amount of timber that, according to the designers, regrows in Swiss forests in 3.21 hours, for them the aesthetics are the key to the long-term acceptance of a structure in society and formed their leitmotif for this project.

The frames

These aesthetics, however, were only made possible through the skilful use of a new type of connector and a good idea from the structural engineers, who had been involved from an early stage. Although they are 28.80 metres long, the frame beams (GL28h) are only 14 centimetres wide despite being 140 centimetres deep, and the almost 10 metre high legs to the frame (GL36), at 14×80 cm, are also very slender. In order to keep the legs this slender, the engineers had to employ a technical trick to relieve the load on them. For this purpose, the legs were given an inward slope during prefabrication so that the base of each one had to be pulled a few centimetres into the vertical position during erection in order to fix them to their steel bases. This enforced deformation generates a kind of prestressing moment at the corners of the frame which cancels out the moment due to the vertical loads on the beam to a certain extent and hence relieves each leg.

The structural engineers used a new type of connection – GSA technology – so that all the loads could be accommodated without damage at the frame corners. (GSA is the German abbreviation for thread-bar-anchor.) According to the developers, this is a structural, interlocking fastening system characterised by high load-carrying capacity, good stiffness and ductile behaviour. Every beam/leg connection uses two special steel straps and bolts at the inside and outside of the corner, plus a threaded bar that joins the upper and lower steel straps together. The threaded bar therefore carries the transverse tension and stops the wood from splitting. The roof elements (with acoustic panels on the underside) make use of double-T panels. These were fitted between the beams to form a roof plate.

In the two-storey part of the building, the suspended floor is in the form of a timber-concrete composite construction with downstand beams made from a combination of spruce/ash glued laminated timber and precast concrete beams. As the largest span here is almost 11 metres and has to carry precast concrete shower units weighing 15 tonnes, the bonded anchors familiar in bridge-building were used.

The use of glued laminated timber beams made of ash (GL40) with flexural and shear strengths at least 50 per cent higher than normal enabled the beam cross-sections to be reduced by about 60 per cent. Minimising the depth of the beam had a positive effect on the entire volume of the building, on the area of the facade, and hence on costs and consumption of resources.

The building envelope is formed by timber-frame elements with 20 centimetre thick mineral fibre insulation and vertical cladding, likewise made of untreated, indigenous spruce to match the load-bearing structure. Around the windows, the cladding opens out like louvres, becomes semi-transparent, allows activities inside the building to be seen, and thus contributes to the delicate overall impression.

Seismic loads – always an issue in Switzerland
An earthquake analysis is always necessary in Switzerland. In order to minimise the loads on the reused timber piles of the previous structure, the designers conceived timber bracing to resist wind and seismic loads. The latter are resisted by a few OSB-clad timber-frame walls in the longitudinal walls of the sports hall, which are designed as shear fields. The frames themselves are responsible for the transverse stability of the building. Cross-laminated timber (CLT) panels have been used in the roofs as a secondary structure and also as resilient shear fields. They brace the building in the longitudinal direction and transfer the horizontal loads due to wind and earthquake into the wall plates.

The two-storey wing ensures that the centre of gravity of the building as a whole lies outside the sports hall. That is why no bracing is required in the 7 metre high glass facade.

Patina contributes to the poetry of this building
In the end, details that are totally matter of course and simple add up to a major investment in ideas and innovations. On the whole, the architecture is rigorous and refreshing – inside and outside. Only the facade might disturb the appearance over the course of time; the cladding turning grey and undergoing other weather-related changes cannot be avoided and will lead to inconsistencies. However, the architects are aware of this. They are therefore continuing the Alpine tradition of accepting the natural changes to wood used outdoors and regard the changing patina as part of the poetry of this building. sjf

In the end, things that are totally matter of course and simple add up to a major investment in ideas and innovations.

<u>Project</u> Sports hall / Regional sports facility in Sargans (St Gallen canton)

<u>Form of construction</u> Engineered timber construction

<u>Completed</u> 2012

<u>Construction period</u> April 2011 to May 2012

<u>Costs / Budget</u> SFr 20.09 million

<u>Floor area</u> 4859.50 m²

<u>Main usable area</u> 2907 m²

<u>Ancillary usable area</u> 753.50 m²

<u>Enclosed volume</u> 32 534 m³

<u>Client</u> St Gallen Building Authority, 9000 St Gallen, Switzerland, www.hochbau.sg.ch

<u>Architecture</u> blue architects & Ruprecht Architekten, 8037 Zurich, Switzerland, www.bluearchitects.com and www.ruprecht-architekten.ch

<u>Site management</u> Ghisleni Planen Bauen, 8640 Rapperswil, Switzerland, www.ghisleni.ch

<u>Structural engineering, concrete & timber</u> Walt + Galmarini AG, 8008 Zurich, Switzerland, www.waltgalmarini.com

<u>Timber contractor</u> Blumer-Lehmann AG, 9200 Gossau, Switzerland, www.blumer-lehmann.ch

<u>Frame & timber-concrete composite beams</u> neue Holzbau AG, 6078 Lungern, Switzerland, www.neueholzbau.ch

<u>Facade & fitting-out consultants</u> Pirmin Jung – Ingenieure für Holzbau AG, 6026 Rain, Switzerland, www.pirminjung.ch

<u>Quantity of timber used</u> approx. 1250 m³

<u>Carbon (C) content</u> approx. 313 t

<u>Sequestered CO_2</u> approx. 1146 t

Good times for fast skaters

The first indoor rollerblade arena in Germany is colourful and spacious. Just four internal columns support the timber roof structure. A pair of 125 metre long hinged girders and forty-four secondary beams carry the roof over the oval track.

The town of Geisingen in southern Baden-Württemberg has had a new landmark since April 2010: 'Geisingen Arena'. It is Germany's first covered facility for rollerblading and offers ideal conditions for leisure, competitions, and training. This project was made possible through the courage of two private investors, a married couple who had long toyed with the idea of adding a worthwhile new attraction to their hometown. Actually, the idea came about quite by chance, as a friend of the couple discovered rollerblading and, full of excitement, told them about it. They were infected by his enthusiasm but quickly discovered that there was no suitable track for this sport in the whole of Baden-Württemberg. And that's how this project costing millions came about.

They needed a roof
It very quickly became apparent that an indoor track would be necessary. On the one hand, the investors wanted to establish a sports facility that would be unaffected by the weather and, on the other, comfortable seating for spectators was also needed, as world championships were planned. Therefore, the arena had to be built according to international standards and rules.

The roughly 7500 m² skating facility, not unlike an amphitheatre, had to blend in with the landscape of the Danube Valley.

Ingenious structural system for the roof
A structure of glued laminated timber beams now covers the approximately 125 metre long × 68 metre wide arena like a grillage on columns. To make sure that all 3000 spectators would enjoy good sightlines, the investors wanted the many perimeter columns to be supplemented by as few internal columns as possible. Using a skilfully selected load-bearing system, the structural engineers were able to reduce the number of internal columns to just four, which are positioned near the corners of the infield.

The roof structure essentially consists of two glulam main beams laid up in parallel blocks (b × h = 42 × 242 cm, GL28c) 26 metres apart; they rest on fork supports on fixed-based internal and perimeter columns, and span the elliptical plan shape in the longitudinal direction as a three-span beam. Arch-type transverse beams (b × h = 16 × 213 cm, GL28c) run perpendicular to the main beams.

The main beams had to be divided into three parts to suit production and transport restrictions, which immediately suggested designing them as continuous hinged girders with zero-moment splices. The locations of the points of zero moment in the middle bay, and hence the hinges, therefore determined the lengths of the main beam segments, which do not match the spans. Taking into account the spans of 30 – 45 – 37.50 metres resulted in the longest segment being 48 metres long.

The main beams were built with a camber to prevent them sagging in the finished structure; their self-weight 'pulls' them horizontal after erection. The situation is different for the forty-four arching transverse beams between 14 and 25.50 metres long: placed at a spacing of 7.50 metres, they ensure that the roof has a shallow curve similar to that of a barrel vault roof.

For architectural reasons, the transverse beams are almost as deep as the longitudinal, i.e. main, beams and their soffits are flush with those of the main beams. The difference in height is merely equal to the thickness

The futuristic-looking rollerblading arena in Geisingen provides ideal conditions for professionals, amateurs, and holidaymakers. The illuminated coloured ring floating in the landscape is visible from afar.

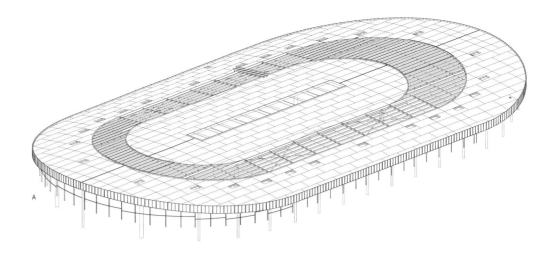

B

C

A → Isometric view of building showing oval ring of rooflights and all the individual roof elements

B → The oval structure is intended to resemble an amphi-theatre and is roofed over by a grillage-type roof made from glulam beams supported on perimeter columns and just four internal columns.

C → Half-section through roof structure; the transverse arch beams connect to the main beams.

D → Prefabricated 'combined elements' with integral glulam purlins. In the curved rooflight sections, the load-bearing ribs of the roof elements extend beyond the elements and are visible. In the finished building they look like separate purlins.

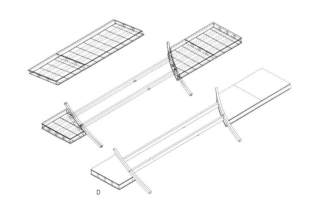

D

of the box elements forming the roof decking so that these in turn finish flush with the top surfaces of the main beams.

The challenge: designing the roof elements

The short construction period from mid-November to late January called for a roof prefabricated to the tune of 90 per cent. The oval plan form and the barrel vault-type section proved to be just as much a challenge for the structural engineers when planning and fabricating the roof elements as it was for the 3D designers: not only does the roof surface curve continuously over the width of the building, but the perimeter windows with the purlins, some of which continue into the closed roof elements as load-bearing ribs, had to be incorporated in the design and factory-prefabricated. There are therefore 146 different element types for a total of 240 roof elements, making nearly every element a one-off. The exact geometries were determined from the 3D CAD model and so could be prepared for CNC production. That work required real diligence, but was essential because everything had to fit together on site; there was no second chance to improve something. With the help of layout and structural location drawings, it was possible to install the right elements in the right places.

Roof decking functions as stiffening diaphragm

The almost 30 centimetre thick roof elements with full insulation, roof finishes, and acoustic soffit were laid on top of the timber structure. Owing to the enhanced noise control requirements inside the arena, the timber contractor devised a special soffit and had the acoustic panels tested.

The OSB panels on the top either overlap or are cut back along the edges so that they create rebated joints once erected, which allows the elements to be nailed together to create a shear-resistant connection and together function as a stiffening diaphragm for the whole building. As the uninterrupted rooflight prevents a continuous plate action, steel X-bracing replaces the missing roof elements.

The offset arrangement of the elements is also important for ensuring the plate action in the longitudinal and transverse directions. The designers chose the dimensions and positions of the roof elements in such a way that together they create the best possible plate effect – at the same time taking into account the permissible transport weights. This led to the development of the layout drawing becoming a real puzzle.

The roof is primarily responsible for the overall stability of the building. However, the perimeter and internal columns also play important roles. Most have a fixed base, but the fixity is achieved in a way that has been used only rarely up to now. The columns are in the form of steel tubular piles driven up to 10 metres into the ground to ensure the necessary load-bearing capacity. After cutting them off at the height required for the columns, they were filled with concrete. The combination of roof plate, columns, and rigid connections guarantees the necessary overall stability for the building.

Perimeter beams as roof supports

Glued laminated timber beams span between each pair of perimeter columns to provide support for the roof elements. An OSB fascia finishes off the roof cantilevering beyond the perimeter beams. The OSB panels along the eaves on the longitudinal sides are rectangular and screwed to the edges of the roof elements. Cutting the OSB panels to size at the transition to and on the curved eaves to the 'narrow ends' of the building proved to be a complex geometrical process; the eaves not only rise here, but every position has a different angle. However, the use of 3D CAD methods enabled these panel geometries to be determined and fabricated as well.

Drainage

Pipes with trace heating are integrated into the roof elements to drain the roof surface. Around the outer edge of the roof they drain the water from the outlets along the parapet to the downpipes. From the oval roof plate, rainwater drains along the rooflight upstand to the four internal columns. Removable hatches allow the siphonic system to be inspected at all times.

Summing up...

The structural system consists of a total of about 600 m³ of glued laminated timber in the two 125 metre long main beams, forty-four arch beams, sixteen curved perimeter beams and 250 purlins in the raised, translucent rooflight area. The architects wanted to let as much daylight into the arena as possible. That has been achieved by installing 2000 m² of transparent Prokulit sheets and rooflights.

The timber contractor produced the entire roof structure in about fourteen days and then erected everything on site. As the work was carried out during the winter, the roof surface had to be set up and weatherproofed quickly – which was easy to achieve with the prefabricated roof elements.

The roof was delivered to site in fourty-two truckloads; three of those were abnormal loads with a maximum length of 52.5 metres and total weight of 74 tonnes. The crews had driven about 450 kilometres with their oversized, heavy vehicles. Two cranes lifted the beams exactly into position on their supports, where they were aligned and fixed by the erection team.

A stroke of luck for everyone

During the opening ceremony, all the visitors agreed that 'Geisingen Arena', built as the result of a private initiative, is a stroke of luck for the town, the entire region, and the whole rollerblading scene. The prominent persons from politics and industry among the guests said it was like winning the jackpot in the national lottery! sjf

A

C

B

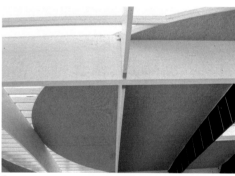

D

Project Geisingen Arena

Client Uhrig Straßen- und Tiefbau GmbH, 78187 Geisingen, Germany, www.uhrig-bau.eu

Design Schoyerer Architekten BDA, 55120 Mainz, Germany, www.schoyerer.de

Architecture CENTRAPLAN – Architekten-Planungsgesellschaft mbH, 79199 Kirchzarten, Germany, www.centraplan-architekten.de

Structural engineering & CAD fabrication drawings Wiehag GmbH in cooperation with kw-holz Ingenieurgesellschaft mbH, 63619 Bad Orb, Germany, www.kw-holz.de

Timber contractor Wiehag GmbH, 4950 Altheim, Austria, www.wiehag.com

Quantity of timber used 600 m³

Carbon (C) content 150 t

Sequestered CO_2 550 t

E

F

A → The first segment of a main beam during erection. It extends 6.50 metres beyond the internal column into the centre span, where the middle beam segment is connected via a hinged joint. The fork supports welded to the tops of the fixed-base columns provide lateral restraint for the beams.

B → Lifting a roof element into position and subsequently fixing it via rebated joints to form the roof plate.

C → Erecting roof elements around the edge of the building

D → The roof elements are supported on the transverse beams and their top surfaces finish flush with the tops of the main beams.

E → Span of main beam between columns: 26 metres. The transverse arch beams turn the roof into a shallow barrel vault.

F → The new skating facility forms part of the leisure amenities situated on the edge of Geisingen.

Wellness under drops of water

'AcquaWorld' water park in Concorezzo near Milan is housed under an enormous timber roof structure shaped like drops of water. Glued laminated timber beams represented the most cost-effective way of forming the irregular structure – and timber is the best choice for leisure pools anyway owing to its chlorine resistance.

Concorezzo in the heart of the Italian province of Monza and Brianza in Italy's Lombardy region now has a wellness 'temple': AcquaWorld. This leisure complex was opened in October 2011. Its main visual attraction is without doubt the dome-type roofs. They symbolise drops of water and are totally irregular in form. A roof covering in the shape of air-filled cushions on one longitudinal side ensures plenty of daylight inside the building. At night, the building shines like a Chinese lantern. The rest of the roof, about 60 per cent of the area of the domes (about 4000 m²) is in the form of a green roof and, from a distance, looks like a hill.

Domes shaped like drops of water

The architects wanted to create a building whose appearance makes a clear statement in favour of ecology and health. At the same time it was important to use a chlorine-resistant material for the roof structure. Timber fulfils all these conditions. Steel, on the other hand, was ruled out from the start not only because of the corrosion problems, but also because it would have required far too much work to produce the many different beam forms for the roof structure – quite apart from the costs and work that a suitable coating would have entailed.

Besides the chlorine resistance, it was primarily the organic form of the domes and the spans involved that proved to be crucial: the building is about 133 metres long in total and about 53 metres across at its widest point. Given the boundary conditions, timber was the only way of achieving an architecturally appealing and technically feasible solution with as few internal columns as possible. These days, the use of CAD and CNC methods means even hundreds of different cross-sections present no problems in timber construction.

Primary structure: asymmetric tripod with intermediate column

The AcquaWorld building has a reinforced concrete basement. On top of that there are curving reinforced concrete external walls forming a plan shape not unlike that of two kidney-shaped tables. Those walls form the supporting structure for the entire roof, which consists of one large and one small dome plus a flat roof joining the two.

The large dome is approx. 84 metres long, 53 metres wide at its widest point and about 17 metres high. Four glued laminated timber arches with slung steel trusses, forming an elongated 'Y' on plan, constitute the primary structure. The two fish belly-style beams are located on

The roof is about 133 metres long and about 53 metres across at its widest point. It covers the leisure and wellness 'temple' in the form of giant water droplets.

the longitudinal axis of the building and form a sort of 'backbone'. A rigid connection joins the beams together above the intermediate trussed steel column.

The almost 28 metre long arch of the end span is supported via a steel pin on the external wall. On the other hand, the beam in the centre span meets the two beams of the 'Y' legs at a node. The latter spread out towards two supports: the glulam top chords and the steel bottom chords are supported on pinned bases on the external wall and the ground slab respectively, with a height difference of 5.76 and almost 4.30 metres. The primary structure functions as an asymmetric tripod with intermediate column, which has been given a white finish by the architects so that the load-bearing structure is clearly visible. The entire framework of fifty-four curved glulam ribs (secondary structure) giving the building its form are supported on this.

Splayed roof structure absorbs roof loads

Self-weight, roof finishes, and external loads such as wind and snow create large forces on the widely spaced members of the primary structure. An imposed load of 2 kN/m² was assumed on the green roof area. That figure includes seismic loads, which always have to be taken into account in Italy.

The fish belly-type timber-and-steel beams carry the tension and compression forces and transfer these to separate supports at the rear or to the splayed timber-and-steel beams forming the legs of the 'Y', whose curved steel circular hollow sections must carry correspondingly high compression. However, those hollow sections are non-rigid to such an extent that they can 'absorb' the forces, albeit only up to a certain buckling length. To guarantee this, the structural engineers have included four diagonals between the top and bottom chords, but – to stabilise the bottom chord – have also provided diagonal steel ties back to the neighbouring ribs.

The 50 centimetre wide top chords of the steel-and-timber main beams are made up of two 24 centimetre wide sections on either side of the steel connecting plates for the diagonals. Boards glued in place fill the ensuing two centimetre gap along the rest of the beam. This was the only way of fabricating the beams with their diagonal connecting plates, which extend far into the glulam top chord.

Ribs form a droplet outline

A total of fifty-four different glued laminated timber ribs was required to create the droplet form. This is because every rib has a different radius of curvature and a depth that tapers towards the support. The free-form curving plan shape also means that the ribs are all at different angles. At the same time, the connections to the main beams are all at different heights, with different angles at the connections. And last but not least, every cross-section was designed differently to suit the particular loads. For example, the ribs below the green roof area have to carry higher loads than those below the membrane roof.

In order that in the end the roof decking could be laid over the entire area without twisting, the top surface of every rib was cut to a different angle which, owing to the free-form surface of the dome, changes continuously over the length of the ribs. In short, every rib giving the building its shape is an elaborate one-off.

However, even the short members between the ribs, required for lateral restraint, all have different lengths owing to the varying angles of the ribs and can only be attached at an angle. A special U-shaped connector with hinges was developed so that it was possible to fasten these members to the ribs at any angle.

Connection between primary and secondary members was a challenge

The structural engineers also developed a type of universal connection for the structural connection between the ribs and the top chords of the main beams. This connection had to be able to accommodate the high shear forces and eccentricity moments due to the incoming ribs at different angles and transfer these to the main beam. At the same time it was necessary to transfer vertical forces from the main beams to the ribs because the primary and secondary members rely on each other for support, i.e. form a complex spatial structure.

To achieve this, the design team took a pinned connection and adapted this to the requirements: A steel plate is let into the side of the top chord and tied back to the plate on the other side of the chord with threaded bars. Two vertical plates are welded to this. These plates pick up the steel plate fixed to the incoming secondary member (rib) with steel dowels and close-tolerance bolts. A pin (d = 9 cm) forms the structural connection linking all three plates.

The entire detail is concealed in a slot at the end of the secondary member.

No intermediate columns in the small dome

The small dome was built using the same design principle. As this dome has more of an egg-shape on plan, a relatively regular tripod of glulam arches with slung steel trussing can carry the roof without any intermediate supports.

The main beams here – similarly to the beams forming the legs of the 'Y' in the large dome – also make use of a splayed arrangement with different support levels.

A→ Each of the ribs is unique and together they span over the base and main structure, although at an irregular spacing, to form the framework for the droplet-shaped domes. Below the green roof, the transverse members between the ribs are closer together.

B → Elevation on the two main beams with their central support and one of the (two) beams forming the 'Y' arrangement with each outer support on two different levels

C → Four glulam beams with slung steel trusses form the primary structure. The tower for the fun slides penetrates the large dome like a tube; structural connections join the 'interrupted' roof structure to the tower.

D → The AcquaWorld roof areas with air-filled cushions have a lightweight look. During the day the transparent membrane allows plenty of daylight into the building.

83

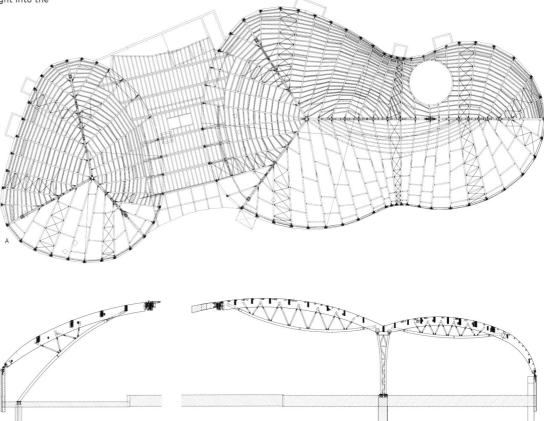

A

B

C

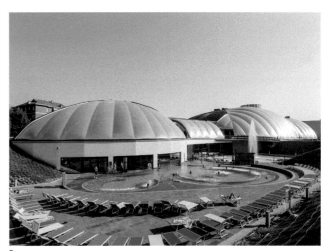

D

Self-supporting structure

The load-bearing structures to the large and small droplet-shaped domes, consisting of primary and secondary members plus short transverse pieces and wind girders in ten and six bays respectively, are self-supporting. The roof decking does not contribute to stability.

However, the structural engineers have tied both domes together via the flat roof, which is at a height of 12 metres and links the domes both architecturally and structurally. The roof functions like a stiffening diaphragm and enhances the overall stability. The idea was to minimise movements within the structure and thus avoid damage to the roof waterproofing.

Slide tower forms part of structure

The tower for the fun slides penetrates the large dome and interrupts the continuity of the load-bearing structure. That called for a couple of additional engineering tricks. The load-bearing members terminate at this tower but are connected to it structurally. So the dome is supported on this tower.

More than 1600 unique pieces

The fabrication of such a complex spatial structure obliged the timber engineers to develop an exact 3D computer model that included all the cut-outs for the steel-connecting components and fasteners. This model formed the basis for the CNC machining of all the timber components. This was where the engineers specified the point at which the arches would be divided, as production, transport, and erection constraints precluded them from being made in one piece. Structural location drawings and consecutively numbered cross-sections, which in some cases were delivered to the building site with each bay packaged together, ensured that all 1645 unique pieces were installed in the right positions.

Foil cushions to avoid condensation

The transparent membrane on the roof structure to the water park consists of three-layer air-filled foil cushions that are pressurised so they retain their form. In contrast to glass, this solution ensures good thermal insulation. Condensation was also considered: when the inner surfaces are warm, no condensation forms even when the humidity is high. That improves hygiene and also reduces evaporation.

The Dyneon ETFE fluorothermoplastic foil is very strong, but at 100 to 200 micrometres thick it is no thicker than a human hair. The foil lets through 97 per cent of the UV-A radiation, which is important for plant growth, and up to 50 per cent of the UV-B radiation. However, the UV-C radiation so damaging to health is filtered out completely, and thus visitors to AcquaWorld can get a safe suntan under the transparent membrane roof. The company that supplied and installed the foil says that the outside needs hardly any cleaning; a good shower of rain should be enough. sjf

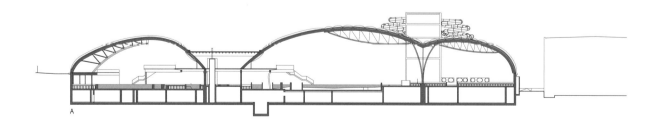

A

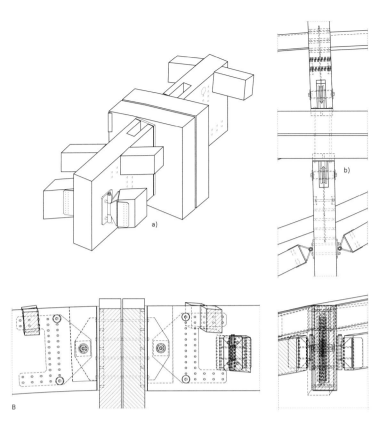

D

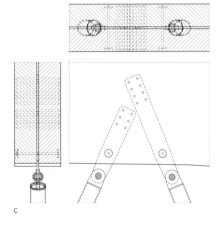

C

A → Longitudinal section

B → Connection details:
a) secondary member (rib) to two-part main beam
b) transverse member supporting roof decking

C → Connection between steel and timber elements of fish belly-type main beam. The connecting plates for the slung steel trussing are fitted between the 24 centimetre thick glulam sections.

D → Wind girders were installed in sixteen bays. The steel X-bracing is connected to the same plates as the transverse members.

Project AcquaWorld in Concorezzo near Milan, www.acquaworld.it

Form of construction Glulam roof structure on concrete substructure

Completed 2011

Construction period, timber structure December 2010 to July 2011

Costs (total complex) €40 million

Usable floor area 5600 m² (AcquaWorld), 15 000 m² of developed area in total, 35 000 m² site area in total

Enclosed volume 69 000 m³ (AcquaWorld)

Client Bluwater spa, 20863 Concorezzo (MB), Italy, www.bluwaterspa.it

Planning Sering Srl – Ingenieurgesellschaft, 20049 Concorezzo (MB), Italy, www.seringsrl.it

Architecture & project management Sering Srl – Ingenieurgesellschaft, Architectural Division, Arch. Federico Pella, 20049 Concorezzo (MB), Italy, www.seringsrl.it

Structural engineering Armalam Srl, 38057 Pergine Valsugana (TN), Italy, www.armalam.it

Timber structural details & CAD fabrication drawings Rubner Holzbau AG, 39042 Brixen, Italy, www.holzbau.com

Roof covering Vector Foiltec GmbH, London, UK, www.vector-foiltec.com

Quantity of timber used 1090 m³

Carbon (C) content 272.5 t

Sequestered CO_2 approx. 1000 t

Leisure pool with sophisticated aesthetics

The building for Les Thermes leisure and swimming centre near the city of Luxembourg looks like it's been cut out of a precious stone. The interior layout is determined by an amazingly lightweight timber roof structure. And wood was chosen not only because it is the best material for a chlorine-laden atmosphere.

Les Thermes leisure and swimming centre is a surprising and unusual addition to Strassen-Bertrange, a suburb of Luxembourg. At first sight it looks like a flying saucer – or at any rate it does when one views the aluminium shingles covering the building on its closed side. The striking shape seems futuristic and piques our curiosity.

An architectural competition in 2004 provided the starting point for the design of this intercommunal swimming centre. However, the winning architects' idea had absolutely nothing to do with a UFO; instead, they saw it as a precious stone that had been cut open, with one side closed and unspectacular, the other side revealing the full glory of the inside. Accordingly, this 'notched' elliptical building is closed on the entrance side, but on the other side exhibits maximum transparency, allowing generous views into the building.

Exploiting the sun and screening from noise as criteria for the building's orientation

The swimming centre's potential catchment area has a population of one million – not only in Luxembourg, but Germany, France and Belgium as well. It contains three themed zones – sport, play, and relaxation – and occupies a site between an industrial estate and an area earmarked for future residential development. The entrance in the middle of the closed facade faces the main road, whereas the large expanse of glass on the other side faces the planned housing. The architects used the spoil from the excavations to form embankments on this side, which provide some privacy for centre visitors.

The building's north-south orientation results in optimum sunshine for the leisure pools inside and outside, while the compact shell design faces the industrial estate and shields the centre against noise.

Timber has all the advantages

As a chlorine-laden atmosphere is normal in swimming pools, the only material suitable for the roof structure of Les Thermes was one that does not suffer in such conditions. So steel, for instance, was ruled out from the start because of the corrosion problems. With major and minor axes of 112.5 and 62.50 metres respectively, the long spans of this elliptical structure were also critical when choosing the material. Under these boundary conditions, timber was the only material that could achieve an architecturally appealing and at the same time low-cost solution with as few columns as possible.

At dusk, the transparent, open side, which is glazed over its full height, enables the colourful interior of the 'notched stone' to be seen.

Timber design dictates half-shell external form

Reinforced concrete has been used for the substructure to this building (three storeys in places). A grid-like roof structure made of glued laminated timber spans the interior facilities. Along the edge of the roof above the closed facade, the roof structure is extended down the side of the building by half-frames that give the building its shape. Rounded, finger-jointed glulam gussets form the rigid 'corners' at the junction between roof and facade. Concrete fins projecting from the basement provide the supports for the timber half-frames. At a spacing of 5 metres (matching the building grid), the half-frames ($b \times h = 20 \times 120$ cm) continue the contours that begin in the basement and create a fluid transition between external wall and roof.

On the other side of the building, the roof structure ends abruptly above the glass facade with its posts and rails. A mitre joint is the basis of the junction with the column here, with steel plates let into the timber plus steel dowels forming a rigid connection. Simply supported purlins span between the half-frames to provide stability and support the roof decking; on the facade there are similar rails for attaching the cladding. Stability for the structure is ensured by wind girders in the middle of the roof and the post-and-rail facade, as well as the decking to the roof structure, which is doubled up at certain places for this reason.

Roof structure with two primary beams and many secondary beams

The roof structure essentially consists of two glued laminated timber beams spanning the elliptical plan form in the longitudinal direction and secondary beams perpendicular to those. One of the two main beams is positioned on the major axis and forms the 'backbone' of the grid, the other is positioned parallel with this, halfway across the rear half of the ellipse. This results in three roughly 20 metre wide bays across the width of the ellipse which are spanned by the secondary beams ($b \times h = 20 - 24 \times 100 - 120$ cm).

For aesthetic reasons, but also in view of the costs, the main beams had to be kept slender, which led to the decision to design them as continuous beams with hinged splices (zero-moment splices). As a column-free interior was the aim, the inevitable intermediate columns were considered undesirable by the architects, especially on the 'backbone'. Nevertheless, the architects and engineers agreed on a minimum number of three columns in one half and two walls serving as supports in the other. The spacings of the columns were chosen so carefully that they disturb neither pool users nor the architecture.

In the end, cross-sectional dimensions of 20 or 38 centimetres wide and 150 or 180 centimetres deep were chosen to suit this solution – dimensions that matched the proportions considered desirable for the 'backbone'. The shorter, parallel main beam 20 metres away rests on eight intermediate columns, which were easy to integrate into the surrounding structure as they are outside the pool area.

Room acoustics

The final issue was how to achieve satisfactory room acoustics. Using acoustic panels on the walls was not an option. Many wall areas were reserved for the red padding that already acts as a 'sound attenuator', but was also chosen to provide a soft contrast to the hard materials concrete, steel, and stone used at ground floor level. So the roof was the only alternative. The architects came up with a solution as simple as it is attractive: rows of inclined panels made up of timber slats suspended between the transverse beams. Not only do they attenuate interior noise, they also lend the roof structure a special character, making it look almost like a sawtooth roof from inside.

Installing the panels at an angle left gaps that provided a perfect chance to allow daylight to enter the leisure centre through the rooflights. There are also large circular rooflights in the middle of the building.

State-of-the-art ecology and safety

Les Thermes is also convincing in terms of ecology and safety. The roof decking includes about 500 m² of photovoltaic panels. A combined heat and power (CHP) system in the building provides the necessary energy and the mother-and-child pool is disinfected with the help of an ozone installation. For enhanced safety, the facility is equipped with a Poseidon camera system with which swimmers in difficulty, even on the bottom of the pool, can be located within a few seconds and rescued.

Light and airy timber structure

The leisure and swimming centre together with its generous sauna amenities, fitness zone, and spacious restaurant was opened to the public in February 2009 – and since then has proved very popular. The architects paid particular attention to ensuring good sightlines and views in all areas. However, Les Thermes is also an excellent example of how a large timber structure can radiate a certain lightness. sjf

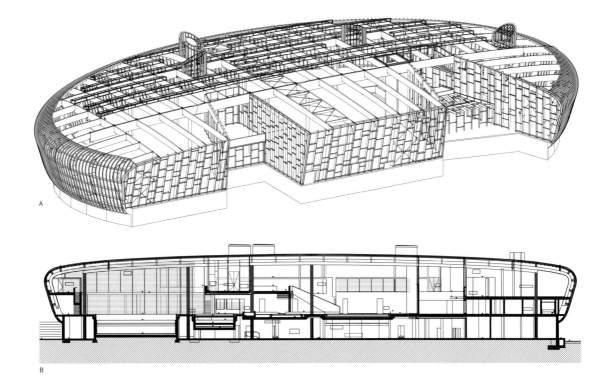

A

B

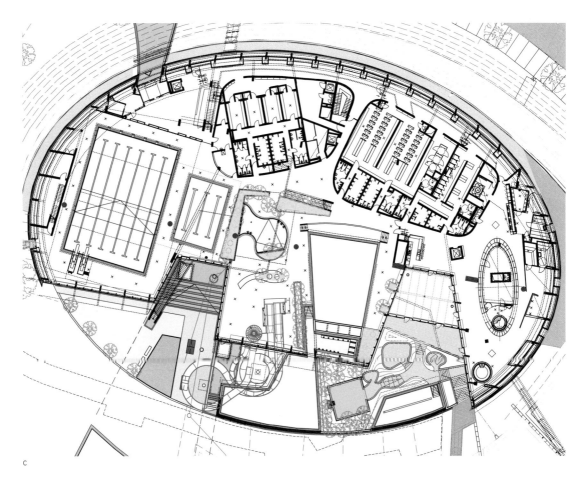

C

A → Isometric drawing

B → Longitudinal section: the 'backbone' to the roof
structure is a hinged girder with intermediate
supports in the form of three columns and two walls
(the latter not shown in this section).

C → Plan of ground floor showing the five columns and
two wall segments supporting the 'backbone'

A

B

Project Les Thermes leisure and swimming centre, Strassen-Bertrange, Luxembourg

Form of construction Glulam roof structure on concrete substructure

Completed 2009

Construction period February 2006 to January 2009

Costs €28 million

Usable floor area 10 930 m²

Enclosed volume 60 560 m³

Client CNI LES THERMES Strassen-Bertrange, 8041 Strassen, Luxembourg

Planning / Architecture Les Thermes architects consortium: Jim Clemes, Witry & Witry, Hermann & Valentiny et Associés (Clemes Architecte, 4221 Esch-sur-Alzette, Luxembourg, www.clemes.lu; Atelier Witry & Witry, 6471 Echternach, www.witry-witry.lu; Hermann & Valentiny et Associés, 5441 Remerschen, Luxembourg, www.hvp.lu)

Project management Axel Christmann, Hermann & Valentiny et Associés

Structural engineering Communauté des Bureaux d'Etudes Schroeder & Associés / TECNA, 1626 Luxembourg, www.schroeder.lu, www.tecna.lu

Building physics / Acoustics Von Rekowsky & Partner, 69469 Weinheim, Germany

Timber contractor Ochs GmbH, 55481 Kirchberg, Germany, www.ochs.info

Quantity of timber used 1075 m³

Carbon (C) content approx. 269 t

Sequestered CO_2 approx. 986 t

A → Glulam half-frames every 5 metres give the building its shape.

B → Rounded glulam gussets create a fluid transition.

C → The closed side of Les Thermes with the entrance in the middle

D → Acoustic ceiling of sloping panels made of wooden slats and vertical slatted panels closing off the areas up to the rooflights

C

D

A stadium as a shining example

The Allianz Riviera Stadium in Nice is unique in many ways. Its roof has the largest timber-and-steel lattice structure (49 500 m²) that has ever been built with such a geometry. The amount of timber used is an advantage in terms of sustainability but a disadvantage in terms of weight, although that proved beneficial for the overall earthquake safety concept.

The multifunction Allianz Riviera Stadium in Nice, which has a capacity of 35 000, was opened in September 2013 and should be one of the venues for European Football Championship matches in 2016. The energy-plus stadium is regarded as a showpiece in terms of sustainability – environmental issues were priorities right from the start.

It took a year to translate the design vision of an organically curving roof structure – providing a light and airy enclosure around the pitch, on the one hand, and reflecting the chain of hills on both sides of the River Var on the other – into a buildable design.

Modelling the load-bearing structure with the help of 3D CAD programmes was relatively straightforward; it was afterwards that the real work began. During the various steps of the preliminary design, the constructional considerations and the geometrical requirements were gradually harmonised so that a series of identical members in a structured global arrangement could be developed according to mathematical principles.

Wood for a lighter structure, better sustainability
The decision to use large amounts of timber in the roof structure was based on three advantages of this renewable building material: its sustainability (keyword: reducing the CO_2 footprint), its high compressive strength in relation to its self-weight, and reducing the dead load of the entire structure, which had a positive effect when considering the stability of the structure in earthquakes, as Nice is situated in a seismic zone.

The design team developed a concept with base structure, grandstands, and a net-like roof structure with two levels made up of a timber lattice and a steel space frame. A membrane covers the entire roof structure. Three-tier reinforced concrete grandstands are incorporated in the reinforced concrete base structure. Cantilevering timber-and-steel 'canopies' provide a roof over this and employ different roof covering materials in different areas. The vertical sections are clad with transparent ETFE foil, which allows the character of the roof structure to shine through and also admits daylight. The horizontal cantilevering sections, on the other hand, are finished with a white PVC foil, which provides shade

The raised perimeter at the base of the north and south sides looks like the hem of a skirt being lifted by the wind. It covers the entrance area.

for the spectators. Between these two areas there are 8500 m² of photovoltaic panels, which generate some of the electricity the stadium requires.

Soft load-bearing structure absorbs seismic forces

As the stadium is located in a category 4 earthquake zone, the aim of the design was to achieve a lightweight, 'soft' load-bearing structure that can absorb horizontal forces in the event of an earthquake. The structural system chosen by the designers has curving half-frames with an inner arch (intrados) of criss-crossing glulam members to carry the compressive forces and a curving outer arch (extrados) made of steel circular hollow sections to carry the tensile forces. An intermediate structure made of steel circular hollow sections arranged in pyramidal form links the two arches to form a spatial truss. At the level of the timber lattice, pairs of steel tubes form the base of each pyramid and connect the ends of the timber crosses.

A total of sixty timber-and-steel frames cantilever 46 metres out over the grandstands at a height of 30 metres above the pitch. They are supported at two points only: at the top of the grandstands and at the bottom of the rear wall to the grandstands, some 2.5 metres above forecourt level. Steel beams running around the whole stadium serve as supports. The lower, 800 metre long steel 'waling' is supported on V-columns that are anchored in the base structure and tie the cantilevering half-frames back to this. There are also horizontal steel beams that tie the peripheral beam back to the concrete walls. The 'waling' takes the tension and compression due to wind, snow, and earthquake loads.

Subdivision of concrete structure and undulating roof

In the event of an earthquake, for the total structure to be able to absorb the seismic forces and stability to be guaranteed, the concrete base structure with its grandstands is divided into fourteen blocks. These oscillate separately and thus dampen the earthquake loads for the roof structure, whose upper support also includes sliding bearings.

The task was to harmonise the numerous individual elements of the concrete structure with the peripheral, undulating roof structure. Added to this was the fact that the grandstands on all four sides had to be raised to maximise the number of seats. The height was reduced at the corners, where sightlines are poorer anyway. That led to an undulating line for the top of the grandstands, which matches that of the roof. Although this varying height is symmetrical about both the main axes of the stadium, it has an effect on the geometry of the roof frame.

Therefore, additional structural calculations had to be performed for each curved section, which, owing to the complexity of the geometry, were difficult even with the help of a computer. Besides the geometry and the applied loads, the calculations also had to take into account the different properties of the building materials, e.g. strength and stiffness, plus external influences such as humidity and temperature, which affect timber, steel, and concrete (creep and shrinkage) differently.

Simulation of roof structure

In order to be able to set up a viable structural model, the structural engineers, architects, and timber and other contractors collaborated right from the draft design onwards – an unconventional approach. The engineers used three programmes for the detailed analysis and verification of the structural model: one for calculating the forces at the supports and nodes, or rather the stresses in the cross-sections and components, another one for the 3D modelling for the computer graphics, and yet another into which all the parameters of the load-bearing structure could be input.

Using the parametric software it was possible to simulate the load-bearing structure as an interactive whole, similarly to a neuronal network. It was thus possible to alter certain basic parameters to change quickly from concept X to concept Y while retaining the coherency of the overall structure, as the programme automatically adjusted all the other parameters to suit. The critical external load was primarily the wind. In total, the engineers investigated 18 million loading cases in the computer and from those selected 232 of the most pessimistic wind scenarios to examine the extreme cases. A further difficulty arose which complicated the calculations: the nodes of the timber lattice are not rigid and permit a certain amount of play.

Low number of nodes thanks to crossing timber members

To resist the axial forces, the designers chose intersecting glulam members of different thicknesses laid up in parallel blocks. The middle of the thicker cross-section includes a slot through which the other, thinner cross-section is 'threaded'. One bolt connects the members at each intersection. This 'threaded' connection halved the number of structural nodes compared with the original plan. The individual members with lengths varying between 7 and 10 metres brace each other and thus halve their buckling lengths; on their own they would be at risk of buckling.

Just the bearing pressure of the timber crosses alone generates compressive forces on the members and hence shear forces between the outer and inner areas. The member cross-sections are sized to carry these forces: the 58 centimetre wide solid timber 'thread-through

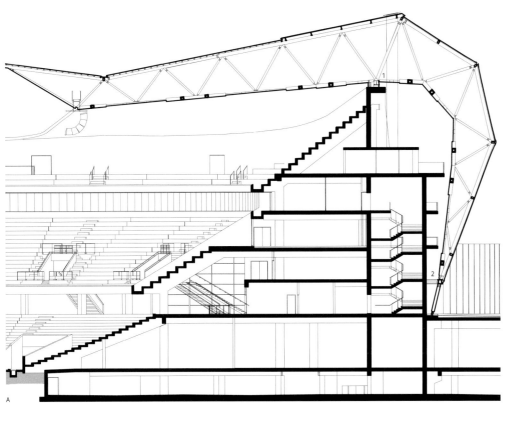

1 Top support
2 Bottom support, anchored to base structure via horizontal connecting members and V-legs

A

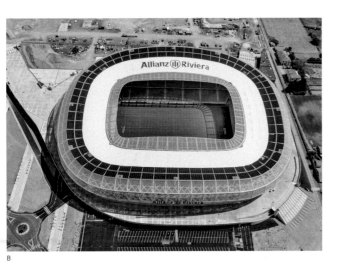

B

Membrane

Extrados in steel

Intrados in timber

Grandstands

Base structure

C

A → Section showing the half-frames cantilevering 46 metres out over the grandstands and supported at just two points. The supports are in the form of steel beams around the entire stadium. The lower one is supported on V-shaped columns and horizontal members tying it back to the concrete structure.

B → Photovoltaic panels for generating electricity, PVC foil for shade, and ETFE foil for transparency

C → Exploded drawing of the levels of the construction

members' are between 16 and 23 centimetres thick, whereas the members with slots have the same width but are between 34 and 50 centimetres thick, and the clear opening matches the thickness of the solid timber member.

Special steel connecting plate

To join the steel and timber members to form a lattice, the timber contractor developed a butterfly-shaped steel connecting plate combined with a tubular steel 'purlin'. Four timber members (via plates let into the timber) plus the steel pyramids can therefore be joined at every node.

The symmetry of the structure about the two main axes means that every timber and steel component in the roof structure occurs four times. Meticulously planned site operations, detailed structural location drawings, and constant fine adjustments with millimetre precision helped when assembling and positioning the curved half-frames consisting of three pre-assembled sections. The sixty half-frames were erected at intervals and joined with glulam crosses, but without the steel super-structure. For erection, the crosses could be rotated just enough about their crossing point like scissors so that the crosses linking the half-frames could be slipped between these and then spread apart again to rotate the connecting plates into line with the plates in the half-frames.

The result is a masterpiece

Designing and constructing complex geometry on this scale can be regarded as a masterly performance. It is the result of optimum cooperation between all members of the planning team, who also understood how to use the very latest software to accomplish this task and interpret the respective outputs of the iterative approximation process. The goal of creating a lightweight, flexible structure has therefore been achieved. sjf

A

B

C

D

A → The timber members intersecting at any one node are all of the same type. The plates let into the timber for the 'thread-through members' are installed perpendicular to the thickness of the cross-section and anchored on the narrow sides with steel dowels.

B → The 'slotted' members are made of four glulam laminations laid up in parallel blocks. The plates for the hinged connections let into the timber parallel with the width of the member are connected via steel dowels in the two middle laminations, which are then covered by the two outer laminations. The two middle laminations are curtailed to form the slot.

C → The glulam crosses consist of one narrow solid timber member and one member with a 'slot'. The former is threaded through the latter.

D → Once in position, the connecting plates of the timber crosses could be rotated onto the connecting plates of the frame by opening them like scissors.

A

B

C

Project **Allianz Riviera multifunction stadium in Nice, www.allianz-riviera.fr**

Form of construction **Engineered timber-and-steel structure**

Construction period **July 2011 to September 2013**

Costs **€243.5 million**

Client **City of Nice, 06364 Nice, France, www.nice.fr**

Contractor **Nice Eco Stadium (NES; subsidiary of VINCI)**

Funding **Private-public-partnership (PPP) model**

Developer **ADIM Côte-d'Azur, 06202 Nice, France, www.adim.fr**

General contractor **VINCI Concessions Rhône Alpes, www.vinci.com**

Architecture **Wilmotte & Associés, 75012 Paris, France, www.wilmotte.fr**

Structural engineering **IOSIS et EGIS Bâtiment, 78286 Guyancourt Cedex, France, www.egis.fr**

Timber contractor **Fargeot Lamellé Collé, 71220 Vérosvres, France, www.arbonis.com**

Steelwork **SMB Constructions Métalliques, 22440 Ploufragan, France, www.smb-cm.fr**

Erection **G.M.G. General Montaggi Genovesi S.r.l., 16128 Genoa, Italy, www.generalmontaggigenovesi.it**

Quantity of timber used **4000 m³**

Carbon (C) content **1000 t**

Sequestered CO_2 **3664 t**

Quantity of steel in roof structure **3300 t**

Further information
**Films (in French) showing the construction of the stadium:
www.tinyurl.com/ka43epo
www.tinyurl.com/ml4jf4f**

A → The PVC foil covering the timber-and-steel 'canopy' cantilevering out over the grandstands provides shade for the spectators.

B → The finished structure has a membrane covering raised clear of a timber lattice. The peripheral steel 'waling' on V-shaped columns forms the lower support for the roof structure.

C → The new multifunction stadium in Nice has a transparent envelope.

Multi-storey buildings

LifeCycle Tower One and Illwerke offices

The LCT One unitised building system could well help modern timber construction to recapture the cultural significance that timber buildings had for towns and cities in the Middle Ages. Two examples demonstrate the comprehensive options of this hybrid building system, which is suitable for both high- and low-rise structures. The qualities of this system are, first and foremost, its standardised industrial production that takes up the early ideas of Konrad Wachsmann and transfers them to the modern age.

It was in 2009 that Cree GmbH, a subsidiary of the Rhomberg construction company, initiated a research project with an interdisciplinary team of experts headed by Vorarlberg-based architect Hermann Kaufmann. Together, the specialists from R&D, practice, and applied science created a new timber hybrid building system that has helped timber construction shake off the provincialism with which it had been occasionally labelled. A rationalised modular system in every way, it can be used to construct buildings up to thirty storeys, i.e.

100 metres, high. The first two buildings erected with this new system – the eight-storey LifeCycle Tower One (LCT One) in Dornbirn in 2012 and the Illwerke office building in Montafon in 2013 – have restored timber construction to the world of international architecture and contemporary urban design.

LifeCycle Tower One
Various factors are responsible for the pioneering achievement of the LCT system. CAD design and

Symbol for a new era in timber construction: the eight-storey LifeCycle Tower One built to the passive-house energy standard

computer-controlled fabrication plant allow the parts of the system, including insulation and space for services, to be prefabricated with millimetre accuracy and delivered to the building site just in time. Consequently, erection can take place straight away, with a consistently high standard of quality and without delays for drying out. In addition, the potential for errors is reduced to a minimum. The degree of prefabrication for the wall and floor elements is geared to future needs. That and the use of the renewable raw material wood, the low dust and noise emissions plus the complete recyclability guarantee the sustainability of this form of construction.

Using the LCT system, one to two complete storeys were erected every day, meaning that, once the ground floor slab and the service core were finished, a weatherproof structural carcass could be assembled within ten days. It was also possible to increase the efficiency of the use of materials and resources, e.g. by using non-encapsulated, load-bearing, solid timber components – a new approach for multi-storey timber buildings. Refraining from encapsulation allowed the key features of the wood – texture, feel, and charm – to be retained and thus improve the interior. Built in reinforced concrete for fire protection reasons, the service core contains the stairs and lift, and at the same time carries loads and braces the building. The external wall construction, with the load-bearing timber structure left visible on the inside, has a U-value of 0.12 W/m²K for a thickness of 48 centimetres. From inside to outside, the layers of the wall are: OSB/vapour barrier, insulated timber frame, cement-bonded wood fibre board, cavity framing closed off with lightweight, incombustible, composite aluminium elements. With no walls or columns inside the building, users can subdivide the interior to suit their needs.

Simple plug-in connection

The LCT system is designed with pinned joints, with the floors functioning as horizontal diaphragms with shear-resistant connections and the facade columns as pinned-end members. There are predefined points on the vertical service core for carrying the horizontal loads of the prefabricated suspended floor elements and transferring these to the foundations. The floor elements at 2.70 metres centre-to-centre are supported on unclad glued laminated timber columns integrated into the facade which carry the loads from the floor elements down to the next twin timber column. As is customary with forms of construction using prefabricated components, the twin columns are fixed to the floor elements and secured against pull-out by way of simple plug-in tube/spigot connections. This principle behind the structural carcass guarantees the dimensional stability of the building in the vertical direction and

ensures that vertical progress proceeds quickly and according to schedule. All floor and wall elements include projecting steel tubes. Each subsequent column fits onto the top end of the steel tube exactly. Afterwards, the spaces within the column footprint are filled with grout. This creates a stable structural connection between the upper facade column and the floor element fitted below. So the vertical progress and the speed of erecting the LCT modular system are essentially determined by the high precision of modern engineered timber construction.

Multifunctional composite floors

The timber-concrete composite ribbed floor developed specially for the LCT system combines various functions and also fulfils architectural requirements. Its comparatively low self-weight is due to the relatively lightweight glulam ribs that are finished with an 80 millimetre concrete topping. As with the exposed timber facade columns, the solid timber ribs of the composite floor are left on show. The multifunctional building services were installed between the exposed timber ribs of the suspended floor elements. Service units, likewise prefabricated, include ventilation, sprinkler, and lighting systems as well as heating and cooling modules. The acoustic performance of the floor has been optimised through the use of a raised access floor whose voids were filled with concrete afterwards. Steel brackets, enclosed in gypsum fire-resistant board (GKF) to comply with fire protection requirements, are used to attach the composite floors to the service core.

The fire protection concept required the individual storeys to be separated from each other. A reinforced concrete ring beam around each composite floor interrupts the glulam facade columns at every floor. In the event of a fire on one floor, the concrete prevents the fire spreading to the next floor above or below via the timber columns. The fire design of the composite floor was carried out to Eurocode 4 (REI). Cree GmbH carried out five series of laboratory tests to establish the fire resistance. Four of the composite floors conceived with different geometries were awarded test certificates for fire resistance classes REI 90 (= F90) and REI 120 (= F120). So the composite floors satisfy all fire, acoustic, load-bearing, and appearance requirements.

Office building for Illwerke, Montafon

The new office complex for Vorarlberger Illwerke AG in Montafon, Austria, was built using the industrial building system field-tested on the prototype LCT One building. The 120 metre long, 60 metre wide and 21 metre high structure – and with about 10 000 m² of usable floor area one of the world's largest timber-based office buildings –

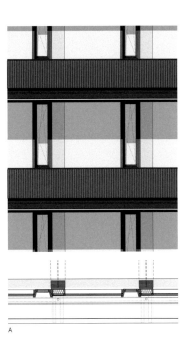

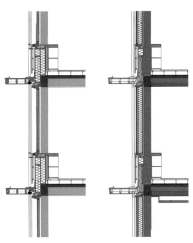

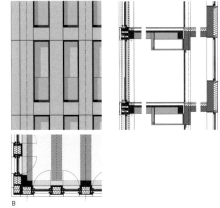

C

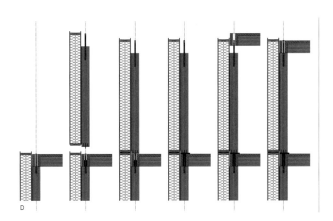

D

E

A → Facade details, IZM

B → Facade details, LCT One

C → The timber-concrete composite floor elements were joined to the load-bearing twin columns via a simple plug-in tube/spigot system to prevent the components from coming apart. This principle behind the structural carcass guarantees the dimensional stability of the building in the vertical direction and ensures that vertical progress proceeds quickly and according to schedule.

D → Erection sequence for LCT One

E → Construction was carried out based on a grid with a consistently high level of quality. The individual components were accurately prefabricated and there-fore enabled both an economic and ecologically sound modular form of construction.

A

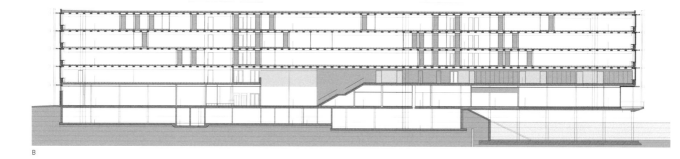

B

A → Modern timber building in classical architecture.
Despite its size, the new office building for the
Illwerke company has a certain lightness about it.

B → Illwerke office building, longitudinal section

combines classical industrial architecture and contemporary engineered timber construction. The building housing the hydropower competence centre blends boldly into the vigorous natural environment of the Alps with apparent ease. It is a stylish eye-catcher that redefines Illwerke's established location, although the horizontal design avoids dominating the scene. The dynamic choreography of the regular pattern of Hermann Kaufmann's facade has sound, economical proportions. Again in this building he has remained true to his fundamental goal of combining industrial building traditions with timber building customs and knowledge. The horizontal lines of the building's frame bring together functionality, delicate details, and subtle elegance. Wood and glass determine the scene. Together they establish a pattern that pervades the entire building. The strict horizontal and vertical symmetry corresponds with the precise engineering and design accomplishments produced in the offices inside. Every unit of the grid represents one working place. Cantilevering floors, clad in copper sheet, ensure a grand appearance. At the same time, they serve as canopies shielding the elegant vertical oak cladding on the spandrel panels below the windows in every storey.

Levitating lightness

Despite its size, Illwerke's new office building radiates a certain lightness, primarily because one quarter of this elongated block cantilevers 30 metres over the reservoir serving the pumped-storage hydroelectric power station, seeming to hover there. Although this 'levitating' building is supported on impervious concrete columns, they disappear beneath the surface of the water when the reservoir is full. This hybrid five-storey building rests on a reinforced concrete basement.

The two service cores are also in reinforced concrete; they project beyond the rear of the building and are clad in perforated copper sheet, creating a subtle contrast with the rest of the structure. Each service core contains inconspicuous lifts but conspicuously spacious and bright stairs that encourage movement and meetings, and extend the communal zones of the office floors so to speak. Fittingly, the interior atmosphere on the office floors is pleasant, conveying a sense of privacy. This impression is reinforced by the exposed, load-bearing, twin timber columns, the built-in cupboards in oak veneer around the periphery, and also the soffits, lined with a total of 100 kilometres of timber slats produced from 76 tonnes of indigenous fir and spruce. The coherent interior architecture is rounded off by the uninterrupted views of the mountains in all directions through the generously sized, triple-glazed wooden windows.

The walls to this building with their timber structure left exposed internally have a U-value of 0.15 W/m²K for a thickness of 48 centimetres. From inside to outside, the layers of the wall are: OSB/vapour barrier, insulated timber frame, cement-bonded wood fibre board, cavity framing closed off with oak cladding. The airtightness value of the building envelope, designed as diffusion-impermeable at the request of the client, determined in a blower door test is n50 ≤ 0.21/h. The heating energy requirement is 14 kWh per m² of usable floor space, which corresponds to Austrian energy performance rating A++. So this building achieves passive-house standard – the first so-called green building on this scale in Vorarlberg, a region known for its timber buildings.

Diversity in unity

The LCT system was developed as a standardised, universally applicable form of construction that, quite rightly, has been established through two important construction projects. Many variations are possible within this open, modular building system. The range of applications (offices, residential, commercial) shows the possibilities inherent in the LCT system. In addition, clients can choose between passive-house, energy-plus, and low-energy standards depending on climate zone and budget. This diversity in unity is a fundamental strategic element. The high degree of prefabrication and the consistent systemisation of the construction process make serial production of the individual modules with high batch numbers possible. Furthermore, the LCT system fulfils one key criterion for a sustainable (building) industry: the work is carried out in decentralised, local/regional economic cycles with corresponding prosperity effects for the region in which the work is carried out and from where the raw materials originate. Cree does not normally export any components. Users are either general contractors supplying the design and construction expertise, and managing the entire building process, or users who take responsibility for the structural carcass as a subcontractor. In all cases, the LCT elements should be produced locally, close to the respective building site, by local contractors using local resources according to the Cree specification.

Primary energy requirement and CO_2 footprint

As was the target in the research project, the LCT form of construction achieves a significant increase in the efficiency of the embodied energy, materials, and work. Therefore, compared with conventional reinforced concrete buildings, it was possible to improve the CO_2 footprint by some 90 per cent. That figure includes the emissions caused by the production, transport, erection, and upkeep during the envisaged fifty-year design

A → Illwerke office building, plan of ground floor

B → Illwerke office building, plan of standard office floor

C → LCT One, plan of standard floor

D → The unclad, load-bearing timber elements create a pleasant working environment in the open-plan office areas.

E → The generous use of wooden surfaces, plenty of light, and the unobstructed view of the lake turn the Illwerke cafeteria into an inviting place.

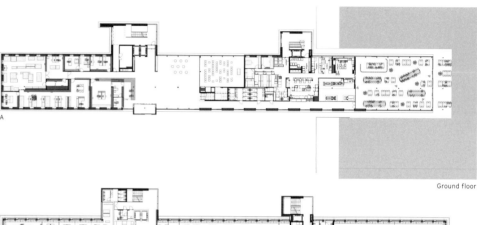

A

Ground floor

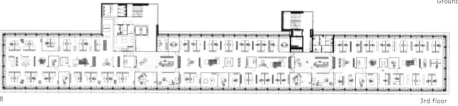

B

3rd floor

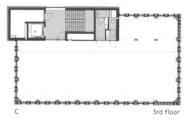

C

3rd floor

D

E

life (including deconstruction and disposal of the materials of the structural carcass). This positive result is partly due to the quantities of timber used: 280 m³ in LCT One – 30 m³ of that in the form of wood-based panel products and the structural solid timber in the facades and the other 250 m³ in the form of glued laminated timber in the composite floors and facade columns. That corresponds to a carbon content (and wood is 50 per cent carbon) of about 70 tonnes, which results in CO_2 sequestration amounting to more than 257 tonnes. The Illwerke building contains some 3000 m³ of timber, which corresponds to about 1030 m³ of solid timber – a quantity of timber with a carbon content of about 257.50 tonnes, i.e. CO_2 sequestration amounting to more than 944 tonnes. More than half of the work involved in the construction of the Illwerke office building was carried out by local contractors and firms based in Vorarlberg. Two-thirds of the timber used was sourced in Vorarlberg, or rather Montafon, and the other third came from southern Germany. mwl

LifeCycle Tower One

Client Cree GmbH (subsidiary of Rhomberg Bau GmbH), 6850 Dornbirn, Austria, www.creebyrhomberg.com

Architecture Architekten Hermann Kaufmann ZT GmbH, 6858 Schwarzach, Austria, www.hermann-kaufmann.at

Structural engineering merz kley partner ZT GmbH, 6850 Dornbirn, Austria, www.mkp-ing.com

Timber contractor Wiehag GmbH (floor beams), 4950 Altheim, Austria, www. wiehag.com; Binder Holz (glulam columns), 6263 Fügen, Austria , www.binderholz.com; Mayr-Melnhof Holz (posts in timber-frame walls), 8700 Leoben, Austria, www.mm-holz.com

Design period December 2010 to August 2011

Start on site September 2011 (in situ concrete)

Timber structure March 2012 (2 working weeks)

LCT system Floors & columns + facade

Completed July 2012

Plan area 305 m²

Net floor area 1765 m²

Gross floor area 2319 m²

Gross enclosed volume 8074 m³

Heating requirement 13.9 kWh/m²a

Building costs per m² €1650

Total building costs €4.1 million

Quantity of timber used 280 m³

Carbon (C) content 70 t

Sequestered CO_2 257 t

Illwerke Zentrum Montafon

Client Vorarlberger Illwerke AG, 6900 Bregenz, Austria, www.illwerke.at

Architecture & project management Architekten Hermann Kaufmann ZT GmbH, Schwarzach, 6858 Schwarzach, Austria, www.hermann-kaufmann.at

Site management Cree GmbH, 6850 Dornbirn, Austria, www.creebyrhomberg.com

Timber contractor Wall & floor elements, oak cladding: Sohm HolzBau-technik GmbH, 6861 Alberschwende, Austria, www.sohm-holzbau.at

Floor beams, glulam columns Kaufmann Zimmerei + Tischlerei GmbH, 6870 Reuthe, Austria, www.kaufmannzimmerei.at

Slats to soffits Frick Burtscher Holz mit Technik GmbH, 6850 Dornbirn, Austria, www.holz-mit-technik.at

Structural engineers merz kley partner, 6850 Dornbirn, Austria, www.mkp-ing.com

HVAC / Sanitary consultants Planungsteam E-Plus GmbH, 6863 Egg, Austria, www.e-plus.at

Electrical engineers elPlan, 6886 Schoppernau, Austria, www.elplan.at

Building physics WSS Wärme- und Schallschutztechnik Thomas Schwarz, 6820 Frastanz, Austria, www.wss.or.at

Fire protection Institut für Brandschutztechnik und Sicherheitsforschung, 4021 Linz, Austria, www.ibs-austria.at

Drainage Rudhardt + Gasser, 6900 Bregenz, Austria, www.rgzt.at

Surveying Engineering Messtechnik, 79418 Schliengen, Germany

Geotechnical consultants Geotek, A-6800 Feldkirch, Austria, www.swr-engineering.com

Facade GDB Fassadenentwicklung, 6850 Dornbirn, Austria, www.gbd.at

Lighting Zumtobel Lighting GmbH, 6850 Dornbirn, Austria, www.zumtobel.com

Net floor area 9900 m²

Gross floor area 11 497 m²

Gross enclosed volume 44 881 m³

Building costs (net) €21.5 million

Costs per m² net floor area €2172

Costs per m² gross floor area €1870

Costs per m³ gross enclosed volume €479

Quantity of timber used 1030 m³

Carbon (C) content 257 t

Sequestered CO_2 944 t

Timber in the city and for publicly assisted housing

Timber construction has been returning to the urban environment in recent years. One example from Austria also integrates the social factor and demonstrates the opportunities for building publicly assisted, ecological apartments.

Donaustadt, a district in Vienna with 150 000 inhabitants and an area of 10 000 hectares, now has a housing complex that sets new standards even in this Alpine country well known for its timber buildings. There are 101 rented flats in this complex: 71 in a seven-storey block parallel with Wagramer Straße and 30 in a trio of three-storey wings at the rear. The roadside block has a ground floor in reinforced concrete (to comply with fire protection stipulations) and above that six storeys in a hybrid form of construction employing cross-laminated timber (CLT). Besides providing structural and fire protection functions, the ground floor also contains social amenities, which are intended to promote a communal spirit and help the entire area to generate its own identity. The substantial roadside building also functions as a sort of screen against road noise and the commotion of the city. The three-storey wings, all completely in timber, behind the roadside block benefit from this screening, likewise the rear-facing rooms of the seven-storey block.

Cooperative construction project with additional funding

With six timber storeys, the apartment building on Wagramer Straße is Austria's tallest residential building in timber. A competition for a preliminary timber design in an urban setting had been initiated in 2009 by Vienna's councillor for housing and urban development, Michael Ludwig, and Wohnfonds Wien, a non-profit-making body promoting high-quality housing in the city. Two architectural practices produced detailed designs from the winning concepts: the Vienna-based architects

Schluder Architektur (seven-storey block) and Hagmüller Architekten (three-storey wings). 'Familie – Gemeinnützige Wohn- und Siedlungsgenossenschaft', a housing association in Vienna, is behind the project and also manages and operates the complex. It trades under the operative umbrella of a cooperatively organised company, Sozialbau AG, Austria's leading private housebuilding enterprise. Sozialbau AG is dedicated to limited-profit-making and publicly assisted housebuilding, and is based on three housing cooperatives: 'Familie', 'Volksbau', and 'Wohnbau'.

The complex on Wagramer Straße is the first time that an urban construction project on this scale has been integrated in a socio-ecological timber construction context funded by the City of Vienna with public monies. The 101 apartments with floor areas between 62 and 102 m² qualified for additional funding from the city authorities which is granted for low-income households and for young families and/or those with many children. This supplementary funding can be granted in addition to the main funding and brings down monthly rents, although this extra funding is coupled to defined maximum income levels and the form of construction of the particular residential building. The funding is paid to the developers, in this case the 'Familie – Gemeinnützige Wohn- und Siedlungsgenossenschaft'.

High-quality materials and construction

Every apartment in this low-energy complex has its own private open space in the form of a loggia, balcony, or patio. There is also a mechanical ventilation system. Healthy linoleum floor coverings have been laid in the

The hybrid front block, which shields the rearward-facing apartments and the residential wings behind against road noise.

A → The standard floor plan shows the long block parallel with Wagramer Straße and the three wings at the rear connected via covered walkways.

B → Section through housing complex showing seven-storey roadside block and one three-storey wing

C → The timber construction concept and the system behind this multi-storey rented apartments complex

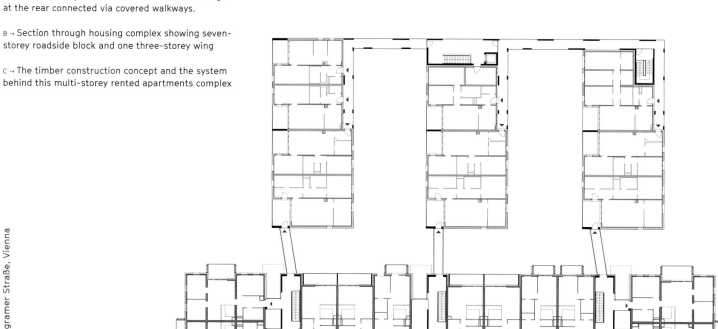

A   2nd floor

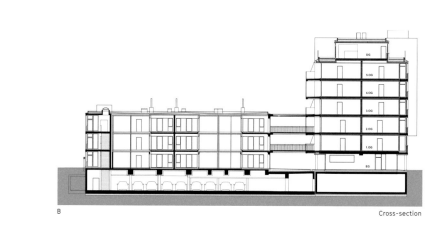

B   Cross-section

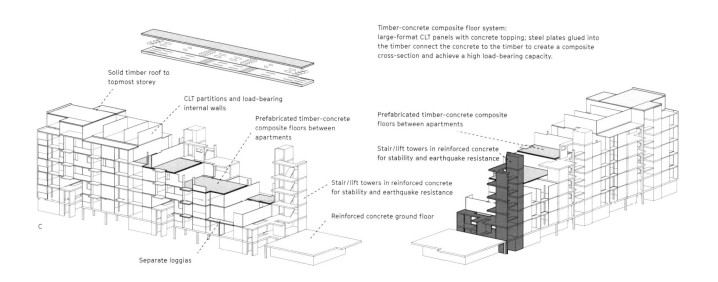

Timber-concrete composite floor system:
large-format CLT panels with concrete topping; steel plates glued into the timber connect the concrete to the timber to create a composite cross-section and achieve a high load-bearing capacity.

Solid timber roof to topmost storey

CLT partitions and load-bearing internal walls

Prefabricated timber-concrete composite floors between apartments

Prefabricated timber-concrete composite floors between apartments

Stair/lift towers in reinforced concrete for stability and earthquake resistance

Stair/lift towers in reinforced concrete for stability and earthquake resistance

Reinforced concrete ground floor

Separate loggias

C

kitchens; besides linseed oil, linoleum contains only saw-dust and cork granules, milled limestone, natural resins, and pigments on a jute backing – all natural substances. Wooden windows and ecologically approved plaster-board have been installed as well. A connection to the existing district heating network ensures a climate-neutral energy supply for space heating and hot water. Such high-quality materials and forms of construction are generally reserved for the upmarket, homogeneous gentrification projects of big, booming cities with populations in the millions and are not found in hetero-geneous conurbations with low and medium incomes. So this publicly funded and cooperatively organised timber construction project has taken on a pioneering role in urban planning. It demonstrates ways of tackling the current problem that affordable housing in urban and suburban areas is in short supply and therefore also makes a housebuilding policy statement. Thus, although young families and families with many children are rare nowadays, they are not forced to leave Vienna's Donaustadt district. This presence of different age groups and lifestyles fosters healthy urban development and a good mix on the one hand. On the other, it enables the vitality of youngsters growing up in town to add dynamic factors in the future.

Time as quality factor

Time is seen as the crucial quality factor in modern building activities. Time-consuming, lengthy construction processes are extremely counter-productive in very dense urban environments with their very closely inter-linked and mutually dependent economic, logistical, and social interactions. Such processes disrupt the overall circulation and interfere with the speed of movement in an area that is thoroughly mobile but at the same time suffers from a fragile transport policy. Therefore, permanent building sites annoy not only residents, but investors, transport planners, environmentalists, and a city's economists, too. It was also for these reasons that modern timber design was chosen for the Wagramer Straße project. The roadside block has six storeys assembled from prefabricated timber elements on top of a concrete ground floor. The structural carcass was finished in just three months. The high degree of prefab-rication enabled a rational form of construction with wall, floor, and roof elements factory-produced with millimetre precision which could then be quickly assem-bled on site so that the building could grow rapidly.

Modern engineered timber construction encourages this unitised modular form of construction and is working towards 100 per cent prefabrication. The great accuracy of the system elements is crucial here because it not only offers unlimited design options, but

also enables a high level of automation during the production of the individual elements.

Building with solid timber elements

The seven-storey block is built from solid timber compo-nents. Both the load-bearing party walls and the non-load-bearing external walls were built with 14 centimetre thick CLT panels with a cross-banded lay-up. These solid timber elements have no voids and exhibit good dimensional stability and durability for a low self-weight and good insulation properties, which makes them ideal for multi-storey residential and commercial buildings. Owing to the longer spans and the fire pro-tection requirements, timber-concrete composite elements have been used for the suspended floors and the load-bearing wall elements are clad in plasterboard. The three reinforced concrete stair and lift cores positioned between the apartments provide the addi-tional protected zones demanded by the fire protection regulations. At the same time they improve the overall stability of the seven-storey block and carry the loads down to the foundations. Bolts in elongated holes form the connections between the timber and concrete, although the final fasteners were not installed until the differential settlement of the blocks was complete. The three-storey wings behind the main block are exclu-sively in cross-laminated timber. Only the access for the upper storeys requires concrete walkways. As the spans here are shorter, solid timber elements could be used for the suspended floors, too. These elements are supported on the party and external walls and continue through from one apartment to the next.

Fire protection learning curve

The fire protection concept was approved on the basis of new technology dating from 2007, which for the first time defined the essential fire safety parameters for timber-based, multi-storey residential buildings in building regulations class 5 (i.e. max. 7 storeys). In line with the provisions of OIB Guideline 2 (OIB = Austrian Building Technology Institute), the load-bearing, encap-sulated components were tested in a furnace for 90 minutes at 1000°C. The components passed the test without any problems and were granted approval. Unfortunately, no test was carried out to establish whether the solid timber components would have withstood the test without encapsulation; the results would have supplied further valuable information. The objection often raised regarding timber buildings in urban envi-ronments is the supposedly higher risk of fire. However, this is based more on psychological impressions than on scientific findings. Fire tests in the laboratory resulted in combustion rates of 18 millimetres in

30 minutes, 36 millimetres in 60 minutes and 54 millimetres in 90 minutes. Even in a fully developed fire, a solid timber column retains its full load-bearing capacity for a very long time before – in contrast to a steel structure – it collapses as predicted. Very often the approving authorities lack experience in this respect. Therefore, preliminary talks with those responsible for fire protection are necessary when those persons are (still) unfamiliar with modern engineered timber construction. Encapsulation increases the cost of construction unnecessarily and robs the building of the look and feel of wood.

Methods of communication in timber

The Wagramer Straße complex confirms the trend towards multi-storey, timber-based (residential) buildings in urban and suburban areas. Nevertheless, it appears odd to hide the warm, natural, and, for most people, positive effects of wooden surfaces behind plasterboard and cement when our towns and cities have had to endure cold and grey steel and concrete facades for decades. It is now time to use the rediscovery of wood as a chance to give our towns and cities new methods of communication. Timber presents opportunities to employ alternative material, surface, and design vocabularies that promise social warmth, homes, and hospitality within an ecological framework. mwl

Developer Familie – gemeinnützige Wohn- und Siedlungsgenossenschaft Reg. Gen. m.b.H., 1070 Vienna, Austria, www.sozialbau.at

Architecture Schluder Architektur ZT GmbH / Hagmüller Architekten ZT GmbH, 1010 Vienna, Austria, www.architecture.at, www.hagmueller.com

Timber contractor Franz Aichinger Hoch-, Tief- und Holzbau GmbH & Co. Nfg KG., 4844 Regau, Austria, www.aichinger-bau.at; Holzbau Winkler GmbH, 3250 Wieselburg, Austria, www.holzbau-winkler.at

General contractor Voitl & Co. Baugesellschaft m.b.H., 1020 Vienna, Austria, www.voitl.at

Structural engineering, calculations & building physics RWT Plus ZT GmbH, 1010 Vienna, Austria, www.rwt.at

Fire protection BrandRat ZT GesmbH, 1050 Vienna, Austria, www.brandrat.at

Building services Team GMI Ingenieurbüro GmbH, 1050 Vienna, Austria, www.teamgmi.com

Project partners binderholz bausysteme, 5400 Hallein, Austria, www.binderholz.com; Saint-Gobain RIGIPS Austria, 8990 Bad Aussee, Austria, www.rigips.com

Landscaping Carla Lo Landschaftsarchitektur, 1030 Vienna, Austria; Quality control by IBO-Ökopass (verification of building biology and building ecology quality), energy performance certificate to OIB Guideline

Usable floor space, apartments 8440 m²

Communal areas 800 m²

Completed spring 2013

Total costs €15 million

Public funds €6.3 million (housebuilding grants from City of Vienna)

Quantity of timber used 2500 m³

Carbon (C) content 625 t

Sequestered CO_2 2290 t

A

B

C

A → The stair and lift cores were built first – in reinforced concrete to comply with fire protection stipulations. They are also responsible for the stability of the structure and for carrying loads.

B → The CLT elements were used for many purposes: as load-bearing walls, encapsulated in the seven-storey building, as timber-concrete composite suspended floors, and as non-load-bearing external walls.

C → The three-storey wings on the quiet side away from the road also employ the continuous horizontal bands of the main block as a facade theme and thus lend the building envelope continuity.

D → Affordable housing with architectural appeal for young families in the centre of town does not have to remain a dream.

E → A compact, housing cooperative development in an exciting overall composition with direct, neighbourhood-style references.

D

E

A milestone in multi-storey timber residential building

The Canols staff hostel has been built on the site of the old hostel at 1500 metres above sea level at the foot of the Parpaner Rothorn mountain in the Canton of Graubünden. It is the first six-storey timber accommodation-style building in which the wooden surfaces have been left exposed both inside and outside.

Starting in the valley, the Rothorn cable cars take tourists via an intermediate station to the western summit, where there is a panorama restaurant and sun deck. Tourism-dependent businesses, like those of cable car operator Lenzerheide Bergbahnen AG, require accommodation for seasonal staff near the cable car stations. In this case an investor has provided the new Canols staff hostel. A total of sixty-eight workers can be accommodated in the thirteen double and forty-two single rooms.

The large volume of this rectangular block fits in well with the existing buildings belonging to the cable car company. This six-storey utility building, made primarily of indigenous spruce, is a powerful statement in favour of sustainability in the Alps. In order that the workers enjoy their short stay in their little 15 m² single rooms, the designers have left the walls and soffits as untreated wooden surfaces. In addition, the building is based on a diffusion-permeable concept, which ensures a suitable, pleasant interior climate. A vapour barrier in the building envelope and mechanical ventilation are unnecessary with such a concept, which reduced the cost of the building and cuts the cost of future maintenance.

Well-conceived interior layout

Although at first sight the number of windows and their size might seem meagre, this is compensated for by their south-west orientation with a view of the Rothorn and the lake at the foot of that mountain, the Heidsee. Moreover, the incoming daylight suits the size of the rooms, and the inward-opening windows of the upper floors can be opened over the full width of the room. The corridors have been kept deliberately narrow without any daylight so that residents do not hang around, possibly creating disturbing noise. The doors to the single and double rooms lead off from the corridors, neatly arranged in shallow recesses that function as small entrance lobbies and break up the uniform lines of the corridors. Communal amenities are located on the ground floor. There is a common room with oak furniture and large windows fitted flush with the external leaf which provide a link with the outside world. The occupants can also cook for themselves or in groups in a shared kitchen, and every room is allocated a cupboard for food and drinks in a separate larder.

Diversity of timber construction

All floors have the same plan layout and so loads are carried consistently and without any discontinuity. However, the design does take account of different requirements and specifications. For structural and fire protection reasons, the stairs/lift shaft and ground floor are in reinforced concrete. These areas also house

The fire stops made from tin-plated stainless steel continue right around the building and constitute a characteristic feature. The building's compact architecture fits in well with the operations building for the Lenzerheide cable car.

laundry rooms, building services and communal amenities for the occupants, which are subdivided internally with prefabricated timber elements. Using a unitised form of timber construction, the five upper floors were then built off this concrete base and service core, which is in the form of an upright 'L', with the vertical leg forming the narrow south wall. A timber frame design has been used for the two longitudinal sides of the hostel, clad on the inside with cross-laminated timber (CLT) in facing quality. On the narrow north elevation, the timber engineers specified a CLT solution to comply with earthquake requirements. An 18 centimetre thick CLT wall, left exposed on the inside and clad on the outside with 20 centimetre thick mineral insulation, is used over the full height of the building.

Local spruce for external cladding

Glued timber box elements have been used for the roof and the suspended floors. These elements are made of large 27 millimetre thick cross-laminated timber glued to glulam ribs, with the soffit boards, like the walls, in facing quality. Such elements are suitable for multi-storey residential buildings because although they have a low self-weight and low depth, they are still suitable for long spans. The voids are filled with a mineral insulation. A fleece, paving slabs, and mineral impact sound insulation guarantee the necessary sound insulation and fire protection for the suspended floors. A sliding detail has been used for the junctions between the underside of the suspended floors and the partitions separating the rooms. The flat roof is finished with 50 millimetres of loose gravel. The building's stability is guaranteed by the service core at the southern end, the CLT north wall, the suspended floors, and the roof. All floors and internal and external walls include mineral insulation. The timber facade that distinguishes this building is made of a single layer of 21 millimetre thick tongue and groove boards made of local spruce. They were given a grey patina in advance by applying a thin varnish because the different sides of the building are exposed to different weather conditions, which would have hindered the formation of a uniform grey colour.

Short construction time was deciding factor

The high degree of prefabrication led to the comparatively short construction time of just eight months. A total of 335 wall and 145 floor elements, including the sprinkler installation in the suspended floors, were factory-prefabricated. During this work the visible, load-bearing CLT facing to the timber-frame construction was glued under pressure directly to the glulam ribs. This therefore satisfies the aesthetic requirements regarding the surfaces – the spruce had to remain visible – and the

structural requirements – the tensile forces are thus efficiently transferred to the timber structure via the glulam ribs. The elements were delivered to the building site just in time and then lifted into position with a crane in quick succession for highly accurate assembly according to the modular principle.

Fire protection – first time for exposed wooden surfaces inside and outside

In line with the Swiss fire protection regulations, the Canols hostel was classified by the authority responsible, in this case the Canton of Graubünden Fire Authority, as a six-storey accommodation facility. Although buildings in this category intended for this type of use cannot normally be built with combustible surfaces and load-bearing members, in this case the authority granted an approval which stipulated a specific fire protection concept for the building. That concept included a series of structural and technical measures, in some instances based on the provisions of the new fire protection regulations, which only came into force on 1 January 2015. The main fire protection measures required by the approval were as follows:
– A sprinkler installation providing full protection throughout the building
– A system of fire detectors monitoring the entire building
– A smoke and heat extraction system
– Construction of the timber external wall, including cladding, according to Swiss Lignum Documentation Fire Protection 7.1: 'External walls – construction and cladding'
– Classification of the building in Swiss quality control stage Q 4, supervised and checked by a specialist engineer according to Swiss Lignum Documentation 2.1: 'Building with timber – quality control in fire protection'
– A safety clearance of at least 7.5 metres to adjacent buildings

Whereas the mineral ground floor and service core were built to class REI 60 fire resistance standard, the load-bearing timber members of the upper floors are class R 60. The suspended floors and corridor walls form fire compartments and had to comply with class EI 60 requirements because of their timber construction, but the partitions separating the individual rooms are only EI 30 because of the full sprinkler installation. The window frames, clad in tin-plated, non-rusting stainless steel, continue as fire stops around the entire building, forming a symmetrical feature, a frame typifying the timber structure, which is broken up by the window openings. This highly visible fire protection measure is a symbolic vanguard for modern, multi-storey construction

A

119

B

A → The compact architecture of the block takes into account the microclimate building situation at 1500 metres above sea level, where it is important to minimise heat losses through the building envelope.

B → The untreated wood walls and soffits plus the diffusion-permeable design result in a pleasant interior climate in the individual rooms.

C → The corridors, illuminated by artificial light only, have been kept deliberately narrow to discourage groups from congregating, avoiding the associated noise; they are, however, slightly wider at the entrance doors to the rooms.

C

in timber which displays this established building material internally and externally, and does not hide it behind cladding and lining, as was usual in the past.

Indigenous, renewable raw materials for structure and energy supply

The Lenzerheide region has a communal heating association that covers the space heating and hot water requirements of residential buildings and businesses centrally via a group heating network. The base and peak loads are covered by two wood chippings-fired / wood-gasification boilers with outputs of 2500 and 1600 kilowatts. An oil-fired boiler and two further emergency boilers are available as backups and to bridge maintenance times. The annual consumption of wood chippings is 18 000 standard cubic metres, which results in a CO_2-saving of 3000 tonnes compared with fossil fuels. By using the group heating network solution, Canols hostel, with a 62 kilowatt connection, saved the cost of installing its own heating system and the associated chimney plus the regular cleaning by a chimney sweep. This construction project and its energy supply policy fulfil the criteria for Switzerland's envisaged 2000-watt society. mwl

Client Avantimo AG, 9016 St Gallen, Switzerland, www.fortimo.ch

Architecture Lenz, Voneschen & Partner AG, 7078 Lenzerheide, Switzerland, www.lv-p.ch

Project management Baumgartner Baurealisation AG, 9400 Rorschach, Switzerland, www.bbrag.ch

Timber contractor Künzli Holz AG, 7260 Davos Dorf, Switzerland, www.kuenzli-davos.ch

Timber & fire protection engineers Makiol + Wiederkehr, 5712 Beinwil am See, Switzerland, www.holzbauing.ch

HVAC / Sanitary consultants Vitali Haustechnik AG, 7078 Lenzerheide, Switzerland, www.vitalihaustech.ch

Electrical engineers ARG Huder / Jon Caviezel AG, 7078 Lenzerheide, Switzerland

No. of storeys 6

Floor area 309 m²

Volume 5550 m³

Construction period 8 months

Reference area for energy calculations 1850 m²

Costs SFr 5 million

Quantity of timber used 280 m³

Carbon (C) content 70 t

Sequestered CO_2 257 t

A → Plan of 3rd floor (typical for all residential floors)

B › Plan of ground floor showing communal areas

C → The L-shaped service core contains the complete ground floor and stairs / lift shaft and was built in reinforced concrete to comply with fire protection requirements.

D → Longitudinal section through staff hostel

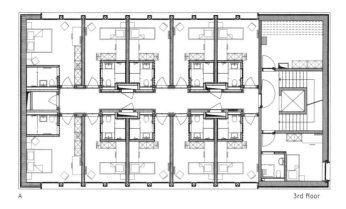

A   3rd floor

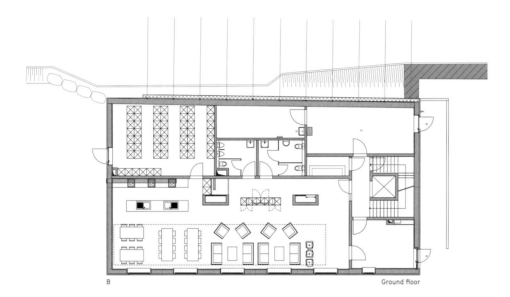

121

B   Ground floor

C

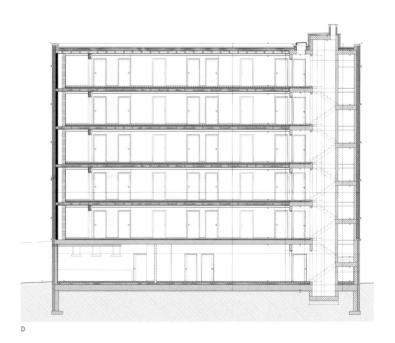

D

Organic timber construction in an urban setting

Wood, as a renewable material, was more than ever a focus of attention at the International Building Exhibition (IBA) in Hamburg. One defining structure integrated this idea into a post-modern architectural setting.

The name says it all: Wälderhaus (Forest House). Inside and outside, it keeps its promise – wood, forest, and an abundance of nature. The asymmetric form of this striking building lends it an organic vitality; it is a successful symbiosis of its usage, its materials, and its design language. Each of the five floors of this 21 metre high multifunctional building steps back to some degree. There are three storeys in cross-laminated timber (CLT) on top of two storeys in concrete. In his design, the architect Andreas Heller heeded the maxim 'form follows function'. The leitmotif shaping the architecture here was the forest – jagged and layered, with the set-back upper storeys reminiscent of the dynamic form and differentiated structure of a roughly chopped tree trunk. With its unusual outline and spatial diversity, the Wälderhaus forms an imposing gateway to the new Wilhelmsburg Island Park. Visitors are treated to seminar, exhibition, restaurant, and hotel functions on almost 6000 m² of gross floor area under one roof. The client, the forestry conservation charity Schutzgemeinschaft Deutscher Wald e.V., uses the building as its new headquarters, refinancing the cost of building by letting the various functional units.

Larch wood facade and green roof

The facade is an outward demonstration of the fundamental theme of wood as a renewable raw material. The curving block is clad in polygonal shiplap boarding made of PEFC-certified, weather-resistant larch that takes on a natural grey patina over time. Nesting boxes for insects and birds have been incorporated in the timber facade. There are also various recesses and boxes for plants. Behind the parapet, plant tubs containing indigenous hornbeam trees provide an apt frame rounding off the building at the top. Some 9500 trees and bushes create a green roof densely planted with essentially natural vegetation – a 'breathing' insulating layer that keeps the building cool in summer and warm in winter. In addition, the layer of plants insulates against external noise to some extent. The plants also remove fine particles and pollutants from the air and their growth through photosynthesis optimises the CO_2 footprint.

As not all of the rainwater is drained from the roof, it can evaporate from the large area of vegetation and thus cool the air and improve the microclimate. This cooling effect also contributes to improving the output of the photovoltaic installation on the roof. Photovoltaic panels reach their optimum efficiency with a solar cell temperature of about 25°C. The energy yield drops by about 0.33 to 0.5 per cent per degree Celsius rise in cell temperature, which leads to losses during the summer months, when yields should reach their maximum. Hot weather causes the cell temperature to rise, and hence its resistance as well, which reduces the electrical output. The cooling effect of the green roof helps to ensure that the photovoltaic panels remain within the range of more efficient electricity production for longer.

Exhibitions, seminars, restaurant, and hotel

'Science Center Wald' forms the heart of the Wälderhaus. This permanent, hands-on, multimedia educational exhibition on two floors gives visitors the chance to experience the forest as an ecosystem and habitat, especially in the urban context. On the first floor, 'Forum

The highly diverse exterior of this building, with polygonal shiplap boarding in larch giving the building its style, reflects the sustainability concept behind the design: a modern timber building with green roof and renewable, zero-emissions energy supplies.

Wald' has rooms available for events for up to 300 people: a multifunction room for congresses and special exhibitions plus three smaller seminar rooms. Together, they constitute an integrated seminar, training, and conference facility for all kinds of educational events, not just those concerned with the environment. The range of services and offers is complemented by a restaurant on the ground floor with regional and seasonal cuisine as well as an eco-hotel with three-star-plus rating on the top three floors. Here again, direct references to the forest theme are a priority. The eighty-two rooms lined with spruce have been named and themed according to indigenous tree species. So every room has its own mini exhibition and a ceiling-high branch from the respective tree, e.g. common dogwood or weeping willow.

Three storeys in solid timber

To comply with fire protection requirements, the ground floor, first floor, and service core with stairs and lifts are in reinforced concrete. On top of that there are three storeys entirely in cross-laminated timber, including the load-bearing members. The wall and floor elements made of certified spruce sourced in Germany, Austria, and Finland have been left exposed internally. Cross-laminated timber (CLT) panels are made of several layers of planks with a 90-degree cross-banded lay-up and can carry in-plane or out-of-plane loads. These solid timber panels are especially suitable for load-bearing functions because their cross-banded form makes them very stable and enables them to carry loads in the principal load-bearing direction and also transverse to it. In addition, the solid timber elements have no voids and so guarantee a safe structure in a standardised quality. Prefabrication of the wall and floor elements enabled the timber construction phase on site to be completed quickly according to a detailed timetable and without delays. The individual elements were lifted into position quiet, with a crane before being bolted together – clean and dry operations. In the timber storeys, the wall construction with its ventilation cavity varies in thickness between 70 and 150 centimetres according to the geometrical configuration of the particular facade zone. From inside to outside, the walls consist of 135 millimetre thick solid timber CLT panels with their joints sealed airtight, a vapour barrier, the prefabricated frame of solid structural timber sections, and twin-web beams with an infill of 200 millimetre thick rock wool insulation closed off with hardboard. The latter provides a base for the diffusion-permeable waterproof sheeting and at the same time creates a water run-off layer. The facade is finished with a framework of solid structural timber sections to which larch sheathing is attached. Together, they create the geometry for the polygonal facade and

guarantee a ventilation cavity for the facade construction. The U-values of the external walls are: $0.15 \, W/m^2K$ for the second, third, and fourth floors (load-bearing wall: CLT) and $0.18 \, W/m^2K$ for the ground and first floors (load-bearing wall: reinforced concrete).

Modular energy supply concept

The ideas of the highly insulated external envelope with its solar-control glass in triple-glazed windows are continued in the energy supply concept. A varied, modular energy supply concept helps to achieve the aim of a low-CO_2 to CO_2-neutral system environment. The connection to the Wilhelmsburg group heating network, which is fed from a nearby biogas-fired combined heating and power plant (CHP), covers the base load for space heating and hot water requirements. Peak loads, especially in the winter, are covered by the building's own geothermal installation. The building is supported on 128 bored piles, 94 of which function as 'thermal piles'. This is a ground source heat pump system that uses heat exchangers integrated in the concrete piles to remove heat from the ground using a thermal transfer fluid. A reversible heat pump compresses and uses this energy for space heating and producing hot water in winter, cooling in summer. This type of building energy supply is especially environmentally friendly and climate-neutral because there are no emissions. In addition, the photovoltaic panels on the green roof generate more electricity than the heat pumps need. On the first two floors the heat is distributed via low-energy underfloor heating to provide the necessary background heating and also via the ventilation. On the hotel floors (second, third, and fourth), the heat is distributed via the ventilation and the heated towel rails in the bathrooms. Some 80 per cent of the light fittings contain economical LED lamps; only in areas requiring permanent lighting have energy-saving compact fluorescent lamps been installed. The public toilets make use of water-saving three-litre technology. Owing to the high natural insulating effect of solid timber, the upper three storeys achieve the passive-house energy standard.

A first for Hamburg building class 5

The building services concept includes a mechanical, individually controlled ventilation system with heat recovery. However, the windows can still be opened – a concern that is expressed again and again in the age of ever more airtight building envelopes. As the client wanted to clad the building entirely in timber and leave wooden surfaces exposed on the inside, too, the designers turned to what was then the new European design provisions (Eurocode) for the fire design. So

A

C

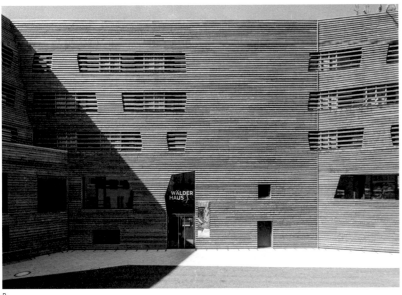

B

A → Unthinkable just a few years ago, but now a reality and the symbol for a new, energy-efficient, and climate-neutral form construction: the return of the timber building to the urban environment.

B → Wood – that ancient building material with its huge variety and its special relationship with people – has returned to the urban setting in the shape of the Wälderhaus.

C → Urban trend with integrated uses: hotel, seminar centre, exhibition, and restaurant under one roof.

A

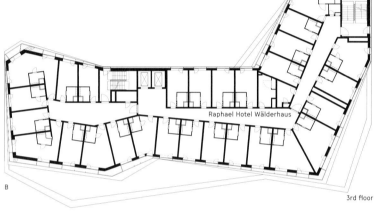

B

Raphael Hotel Wälderhaus

3rd floor

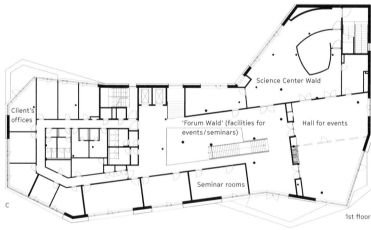

C

Client's offices

Science Center Wald

'Forum Wald' (facilities for events / seminars)

Hall for events

Seminar rooms

1st floor

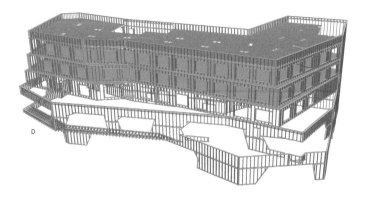

D

A → The organic architecture theme of this hybrid structure finds a logical continuation inside the seminar and conference rooms.

B → Plan of 3rd floor

C → Plan of 1st floor

D → The computer graphic shows the geometrically diverse form of the structure.

the Wälderhaus was the first structure in class 5 (>13 m high) of Hamburg's building regulations with an external envelope and upper floors in timber. By applying the Eurocode it was possible to use specific methods of analysis to assess the structure's behaviour in fire (rate of combustion of the wood) and therefore verify the necessary 90-minute (F90) fire resistance of the load-bearing structure. In addition, it was possible to use constructional measures to minimise the risk of a fire spreading from one area of the facade to another. Finally, exposed wooden surfaces inside the building were finished with an intumescent paint and the entire complex equipped with a sprinkler installation, as is common practice in urban buildings internationally. mwl

Developer Schutzgemeinschaft Deutscher Wald, Landesverband Hamburg e.V., 21109 Hamburg, Germany, www.sdw-hamburg.de

Architecture/Design Studio Andreas Heller GmbH Architects & Designers, 20457 Hamburg, Germany, www.andreas-heller.de

Timber contractor 1 Heinrich Haveloh GmbH, 48683 Ahaus-Alstätte, Germany; (structural timber to 2nd, 3rd & 4th floors, timber facade to whole building), www.haveloh.de

Timber contractor 2 MetsäWood Merk GmbH, 86551 Aichach, Germany (fabrication of CLT elements for Heinrich Haveloh GmbH), www.metsawood.com

Structural engineering Assmann Beraten + Planen GmbH, 22297 Hamburg, Germany, www.assmann.info

Building services Schlüter + Thomsen Ingenieurgesellschaft mbH & Co. KG, 24537 Neumünster, Germany, www.schlueterthomsen.de

Landscaping WES GmbH Landschaftsarchitektur, 22303 Hamburg, Germany, www.wes-la.de

Fire protection HAHN Consult Ingenieurgesellschaft für Tragwerksplanung und Baulichen Brandschutz mbH, 22303 Hamburg, Germany, www.hahn-consult.de

Size of plot 2130 m²

Area covered by building 1360 m²

Gross floor area 5910 m²

Gross volume 22490 m³

Costs €17 million

Quantity of timber used 1386 m³

Carbon (C) content 347 t

Sequestered CO_2 1273 t

Sustainable building in an urban environment

The world's first multi-storey, solid timber building intended for an urban setting was built at the International Building Exhibition (IBA) in Hamburg. About 90 per cent of the 'Woodcube' is pure timber, and neither surfaces nor structure are hidden.

The timber buildings renaissance has reached our towns and cities. When it comes to timber construction, Hamburg has had little experience up to now. So this new building opens up new opportunities provided by the IBA's socio-ecological orientation. The 15 metre high timber cube contains eight apartments with floor areas between 70 and 190 m² on five storeys.

A new idea in post-modern urban planning

The idea of the Woodcube evolved out of an architectural competition. The design by the Institut für urbanen Holzbau (IFUH, urban timber building institute), headed by Philipp Koch, was selected to be built at the IBA in Hamburg. Initiator and project developer Matthias Korff took on this building project, which has resulted in the first fully ecological, solid timber, five-storey structure. He appointed Architekturagentur Stuttgart to modify the original hybrid design and remove all foil, sheeting, encapsulation, building chemicals, paints, glues, and man-made insulating materials from the timber structure. Any risks to health and the environment due to harmful substances in the construction were therefore ruled out. The result is an almost revolutionary structure for an urban setting. The building, including all floors, consists exclusively of untreated, dried, sawn, and planed wood that has been left exposed internally and externally – a new idea in post-modern urban planning.

Stable structural connection

The Woodcube was constructed using the Austrian Thoma Holz100 system of prefabricated wall, floor, and roof elements. Owing to the high degree of prefabrication, it was possible to erect the timber structural carcass within four weeks. The solid timber elements were positioned on the basement around the central stair and lift core (built in reinforced concrete to satisfy fire protection requirements and to brace the entire building). Each element consists of four substantial layers of boards made of spruce and fir. Various board layers are laid horizontally, vertically, and diagonally either side of a layer of 80 millimetres squared sections to form compact building components. The 24 millimetre thick boards are fixed with relatively dry beech dowels that, lightly moistened, are pressed hydraulically into the layers of boards. Afterwards, the dowels swell, tightening them in the direction of the marginally more moist softwood. Owing to the different moisture contents of the hardwood dowels and the softwood boards, a stable structural connection ensues throughout the entire component.

Building with a single material

The walls to the Woodcube are 32 centimetres thick (including a 3 centimetre thick layer of wood fibre insulating board). Protected between two layers of boards, the cellulose-based facade sheathing and wood fibre insulating board ensure the necessary airtightness. Weather-resistant facade cladding made of untreated larch constitutes the external envelope. Narrow framing

The Woodcube is the first multi-storey, solid timber residential building designed for an urban environment in which the timber surfaces and timber structure are left exposed inside and outside.

behind this guarantees the obligatory ventilation. So the entire building envelope to the Woodcube is made of wood and wood fibres. This natural, untreated, puristic form of construction deliberately avoids all adhesives, nails, metal fasteners, foil, and plastic sheeting in its wall and floor elements. By using just one single material, wood, this building avoids the problems that can occur in buildings employing more than one material, e.g. mould growth, condensation, or errors at connections between the different materials of different trades. But no metal at all is not quite possible: metal angles, bolts, screws, and nails are required to fix the elements to the ground floor slab.

Stationary layer of air

The Holz100 elements guarantee a high level of thermal insulation. This is ensured by the naturally good insulating properties of solid timber, with its low thermal conductivity, but also by the air inclusions between the individual layers of boards, which are created by cutting small longitudinal grooves in the timber. Once the grooved layers of wood are assembled to form solid timber elements, the ends are sealed with a mixture of natural oil and sawdust. The result is a 'stationary layer of air' that increases the insulating effect of the overall element without increasing its weight. The Woodcube's wall construction complies with the low-energy standard. The thermal conductivity of the grooved layers of boards is just 0.079 W/mK compared with the 0.13 W/mK of softwood without grooves – a record. The U-value of the wall is 0.19 W/m²K. The solid floors and external walls also guarantee structural stability.

One constructional feature demonstrates the opportunities of modern timber buildings: the 23 centimetre thick suspended timber floors and the balcony floors are one and the same element; it extends from the reinforced concrete core across the interior and passes through the external walls, without forming a thermal bridge, since timber has such a poor thermal conductivity.

As the loads are carried by the external walls, no further columns or load-bearing walls are needed inside the building, which means that floor layouts can be designed to suit individual requirements. Therefore, lightweight, metal-framed partitions filled with acoustic, mineral insulation and finished with gypsum fibreboard were chosen for the interior because they occupy little space and can be moved around or even taken down completely to suit changing interior requirements.

Holistic building philosophy

The Woodcube more or less reaches the passive-house energy standard and is 22 per cent lower than the requirements needed to qualify for funding under the KfW 40 energy-efficient house programme. It not only takes account of the known funding criteria of Germany's KfW development bank and the certification criteria of the German Sustainable Building Council (DGNB), which it fulfils easily, but also sets completely new standards with its holistic building philosophy. The solid timber prototype achieves a CO_2-neutral life cycle assessment that is exemplary in terms of the closed process chain evaluated in this instance – from the production of all materials used in the building to the construction process itself and the building's usage right up to deconstruction (including recycling). That essentially distinguishes it from Germany's legally valid but not all-embracing Energy Conservation Act, which only considers the energy consumption of the building during its period of use. The embodied (grey) energy required for producing, transporting, and recycling the building materials remains unconsidered. Matthias Korff did not want to limit his evaluation in the same way. He appointed the ina Planungsgesellschaft, a spin-off of Darmstadt University's Design & Energy-Efficient Building Department, to include all the important – yet unprescribed – parameters in the life cycle assessment of the Woodcube. The analysis was carried out according to the stipulations of the DGNB certification system. And the result shows that both the construction and the operation of the Woodcube are CO_2-neutral and free from pollutants.

Interior climate and healthy living

The cradle-to-cradle system behind the single-material, unitised form of construction from Austria has earned it a gold certificate from the Cradle to Cradle Products Innovation Institute. In addition, the timber used is sourced from sustainable forests and harvested in the winter during a waning moon phase. The higher density and pest-resistance of this type of wood has been confirmed by ETH Zurich. All the materials used in the timber cube can be fully recycled, are biodegradable, and are unobjectionable in building biology terms. The occupants benefit from this as well as from the interior climate, which in a solid timber building varies over the ideal relative humidity range of thirty-five to fifty-five per cent. This is because solid, untreated timber is diffusion-permeable, i.e. it absorbs excess moisture from the air, stores this and only releases it back into the interior air as required, or discharges it outside in the event of saturation.

Throughout this building with 900 m² floor area, a networked energy management system minimises and optimises consumption and matches it to the behaviour of individual users. For example, the heating, decentralised ventilation with heat recovery and window blinds are controlled automatically, even switched off completely when the occupants are absent for longer. The

A

B

A → The relative humidity inside a diffusion-permeable, solid timber building varies between thirty-five and fifty-five per cent – the range in which human beings feel comfortable.

B → To comply with fire protection requirements, the lift and stairs core was built in reinforced concrete.

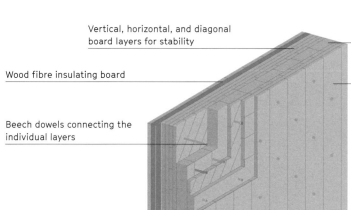

Vertical, horizontal, and diagonal board layers for stability

Wood fibre insulating board

Beech dowels connecting the individual layers

Load-bearing core (vertical)

Sheathing (spruce/fir)

A

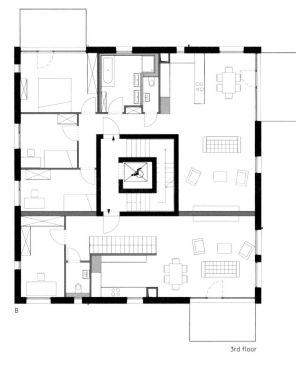

B

3rd floor

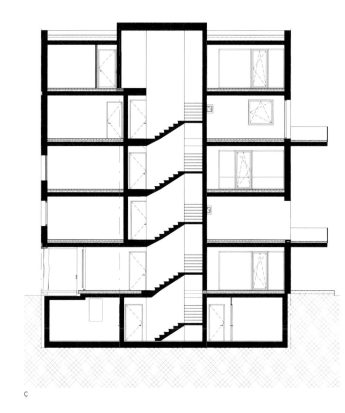

C

A → The walls of the Woodcube, including 3 centimetre thick wood fibre insulating boards, are 32 centimetres thick and, with a U-value of 0.19 W/m²K, achieve low-energy standard.

B → Plan of 3rd floor; the non-load-bearing lightweight partitions can be repositioned, even completely removed, to suit occupants' needs.

C → Section through Woodcube

D → The high degree of prefabrication of the solid timber floor elements enabled the structural timber carcass to be erected in a short time and without excessive noise or dust.

E → The air-filled grooves between the layers of boards improve the insulating effect of the solid timber elements without increasing their weight or volume.

F → The timber floor, wall and roof elements are grouped around the central reinforced concrete stair and lift core.

consumption figures of every individual energy consumer, including lights, are logged in a terminal so that all occupants know their electricity consumption and can try to reduce this if necessary. Communal areas such as basement, lobby, and stairs are illuminated with 1 watt LED lamps and the lift is fitted with a braking energy recovery system.

Fire protection requirements more than satisfied
One intrinsic component in the philosophy of the Wood-cube is not encapsulating the wood or concealing it behind facades made of other materials or covering it with intumescent paint or installing expensive sprinklers. And that was exactly what Hamburg's 1995 fire protection regulations called for. However, a team from Darmstadt University led by Prof. Karsten Tichelmann was appointed by the developer to carry out their own fire tests to prove that the solid timber structure does not require any fire protection measures. The tests established that the fire resistance of the solid timber elements is three to five times longer than that of concrete or clay brick structures. The 90 minute (F90) fire resistance (uninterrupted exposure at 1000°C) required for building regulations class 4 was achieved without any problems; indeed, the special prototype design even achieved F180 standard – which could be a record. Therefore, the timber elements in the Woodcube could remain uncovered, and sprinklers or intumescent paint were unnecessary. mwl

D

E

F

Developer Woodcube Hamburg GmbH, Hamburg (D), www.woodcube-hamburg.de

Project development DeepGreen Development GmbH, 21109 Hamburg, Germany, www.deepgreen-development.com

Design Institut für urbanen Holzbau, 10963 Berlin, Germany, www.ifuh.org

Architecture Architekturagentur Stuttgart, 70176 Stuttgart, Germany, www.architekturagentur.de

Timber contractor Erwin Thoma Holz GmbH, 5622 Goldegg, Austria, www.thoma.at

Structural engineering Ingenieurbüro Isenmann, 77716 Haslach, Germany, www.isenmann-ingenieure.de

Building biology consultant Wilfried Schmidt / Ökoplan, 78166 Donaueschingen, Germany, www.oeko-plan.de

Building services Inhaus GmbH, 47057 Duisburg, Germany, www.inhaus-gmbh.de

Fire protection Tichelmann & Barillas TSB Ingenieurgesellschaft, 64285 Darmstadt, Germany, www.tsb-ing.de

Life cycle assessment ina Planungsgesellschaft mbH, 64283 Darmstadt, Germany, www.i-na.de

Volume of building V = 3430 m³

Surface area A = 1474 m²

A/V ratio A/V = 0.43

Usable floor area AN = 998 m²

Transmission heat losses $HT' = 0.246 \, W/m^2K$

Heating requirement $Qh'' = 18 \, kWh/m^2a$

Final energy requirement $QE'' = 39.3 \, kWh/m^2a$

Final energy QE = 39 200 kWh/a

Primary energy requirement $QP'' = 21.3 \, kWh/m^2a$

KfW 40 limiting value $QP'' = 27.2 \, kWh/m^2a$ (22 per cent lower)

Further features Ventilation system with heat recovery, Regenerative district heating supply, Summertime thermal performance to DIN E 4108-2:2011-10, PLC bus cables free from PVC and halogens, Lift with braking energy recovery, Photovoltaic installation, Centralised energy management, Smart metering

Costs €2.6 million

Quantity of timber used 500 m³

Carbon content (C) 125 t

Sequestered CO_2 458 t

Infill developments and additional storeys

c13

TM50

Timber building in Berlin with urban sophistication

c13 is a seven-storey timber building with three interlinked blocks in Berlin's Prenzlauer Berg district. The Berlin-based architects Kaden und Partner were responsible for the design. The building brings together many quality aspects, including architecture, structural engineering, infill development, and building a community.

The irregular facade design adheres to a modular principle. Individual functional units are readily discernible, e.g. large, rectangular windows alternate with small, playful openings, which lend the building an obvious lightness that continues in the white walls of the building.

Offset oriel windows and lightwells
In their design, the architects make references to the buildings of this area built during the *Gründerzeit* epoch (1870–1920), but without succumbing to an unoriginal historicism. Their c13 design succeeds in capturing the historic building context but incorporating it in a 21st century design language. The oriel windows typical of the sumptuous facades of the *Gründerzeit* period usually begin at the first floor and continue uninterrupted to the roof. Here, however, they are featured in the form of large modular windows projecting from the facade but offset to left or right in each storey. This interpretation of the oriel window has enabled the architects to integrate and underscore the architecture of the existing buildings while highlighting an urban form of construction that does not seek to eschew the significance of the past, but instead is able to supply its own, vigorous statements.

The narrow, elongated plot is framed by an old brick school building on the left and a typical *Gründerzeit* building on the right, whose side wing has a fire wall continuing to the back of the plot. However, the new building has not been built up against this wall as is normally the case when closing gaps in the streetscape. This was because the client, 'Stiftung für Bildung.Werte.Leben', a foundation dedicated to giving people a worthwhile perspective through education, had included light and transparency as important aspects in the specification. So in some places there is a gap of up to 5 metres between the new building and the fire wall. That led to the formation of separate inner courtyards with diagonal views which provide extra light gains in what would normally be a completely closed side.

Cross-laminated timber and timber panels
c13 consists of three blocks with different heights and different forms of timber construction employing spruce and fir. Whereas the seven-storey main block at the front of the plot makes use of solid cross-laminated timber (CLT), the blocks behind that, with four storeys in the middle and five at the rear, are built of timber panels. The load-bearing frame for the timber panels was supplied

Whereas the seven-storey front block makes use of CLT, the blocks behind that, with four storeys in the middle and five at the rear, are built of timber panels; all the blocks on this deep plot rest on a reinforced concrete basement garage.

complete with factory-fitted insulation and sheathing on both sides for stability plus cavities for pipes and cables. The stability of the whole building is ensured by the internal and external timber walls. In addition, the solid CLT walls even carry the loads of the external reinforced concrete stairs/lift tower. Load-bearing timber-concrete composite floors are used between the apartments. These span between a grid of steel beams on timber columns over the entire depth of the building (45 metres). The suspended floors are made of edge-fastened timber elements 14 centimetres deep plus a 10 centimetre concrete topping. The wooden soffits of light-coloured spruce have been left exposed and create a pleasant atmosphere in the interior. The entire timber structure is based on CAD-designed CLT, timber panels, and timber-concrete elements prefabricated with millimetre accuracy on modern machines.

Timber building in Berlin building class 5

All the wall and floor components were delivered to the building site just in time and lifted into position by crane. Only the concrete topping to the timber-concrete composite floors was cast in situ to suit logistical and constructional requirements. It took only three months to erect the entire building – and two months of that was due to interruptions to let the concrete cure. Whereas the two timber panel blocks fall under building regulations class 4, the seven CLT storeys at the front are class 5 because of the total height of 22 metres. Class 5 is only for structures in which the load-bearing and bracing walls and columns comply with the F90-AB fire resistance requirements, i.e. upon exposure to fire, the stability or integrity of components must be guaranteed for at least 90 minutes. In order to take account of the fire protection required for both types of timber construction, the external walls, main columns, and the CLT walls required for stability are encased in a double layer of gypsum fibreboard to class $K^2$60. A fire detector system, external stairs, and reinforced concrete lift shaft complete the fire protection concept.

Structural engineering from Switzerland

Architectural practice Kaden und Partner is the co-initiator of a research project on tall timber residential buildings in urban locations ('3H: Holz-Hoch-Hausbau im urbanen Raum'), which is headed by Prof. Dr.-Ing. Volker Schmid from Berlin University's Chair of Design of Composite Structures, Institute of Structural Engineering. This project is concerned with the design and construction of timber-based buildings with up to twelve storeys. 'Interlocking' the CLT walls with the timber-concrete composite floors in c13, which increases the stiffness of the bracing arrangement and also prevents the different materials

displacing each other, is regarded by Prof. Schmid as innovative from the structural engineering viewpoint. The interlocking was developed by Swiss engineering consultants Pirmin Jung and is based on cut-outs machined in the underside of each CLT wall element, similar to the notches in timber-concrete composite floors. These cut-outs in the timber wall were filled with concrete at the same time as concreting the composite floors. This detail improved the connection between timber wall and composite floor, as well as its stiffness, especially when compared with nailed connections.

CO_2 sequestration instead of emissions

The walls to the seven-storey front block are up to 34 centimetres thick; from inside to outside they consist of a double layer of 18 millimetre thick gypsum fibreboard attached to the load-bearing CLT elements with thicknesses between 9.5 and 20 centimetres, followed by a vapour barrier plus more gypsum fibreboard before the layer of 10 centimetre thick mineral external wall insulation in board form with a high density of 70 kg/m³, which is then finished with a mineral render. In total, the building envelope around the heated parts of the building has an average U-value of 0.534 W/m²K. A gas-fired boiler provides the heat for the low-energy underfloor heating on all floors and all the hot water requirements for this timber-based hybrid structure built off a reinforced concrete basement with car parking. Mechanical ventilation, aluminium sunblinds on the south side, and floor-to-ceiling triple-glazed wooden windows in some areas round off the energy concept. A total of 600 m³ of timber was used for c13. That corresponds to a carbon content (and wood is 50 per cent carbon) of 150 tonnes, which results in CO_2 sequestration amounting to more than 550 tonnes. In total, c13 stores more CO_2 than was given off during its construction.

Revitalising the local community

This seven-storey building also makes its mark on the urban surroundings by bringing together the existential functions of living, working, leisure, and culture – separated since the war – under one roof again. The alternating facade structures reflect the mixed usage (housing, counselling, healthcare). The attractive outline of this hybrid structure is inviting, augurs openness and transparency, and makes us curious. Communication, working, and learning take place here; users benefit from advice and therapy, can eat and relax here, live here – together. In addition, the foundation paid special attention to cross-generation, long-term development. The educational work and family counselling based on Christian values plus support for young people is organised with the coming three or four generations

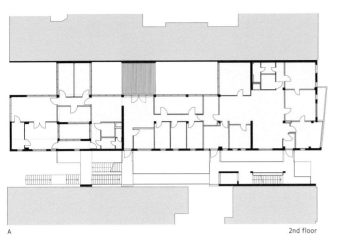

A   2nd floor

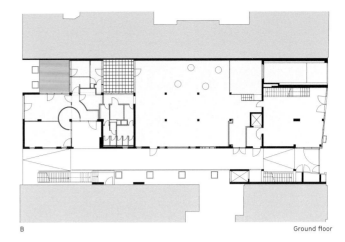

B   Ground floor

A → The holistic concept includes an occupational therapy/physiotherapy surgery, which occupies about 60 per cent of the 2nd floor and is complemented by a paediatric surgery at the front, street end of the building.

B → Whereas the upper floors are reserved for apartments, the ground floor has commercial functions: a restaurant bordering the street, the building's own events area in the middle and, shielded from the road, a child daycare amenity with playground at the rear, northern end.

C → Fire protection can look good: external stairs and lift shaft in reinforced concrete.

C

A

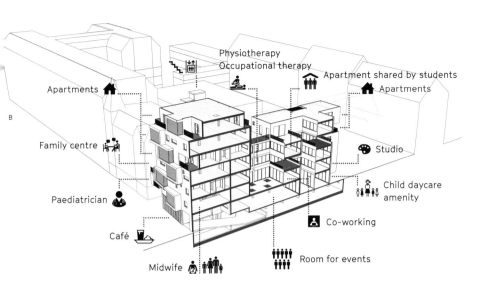

Physiotherapy
Occupational therapy

Apartment shared by students

Apartments

Apartments

Family centre

Studio

Paediatrician

Child daycare amenity

Co-working

Café

Room for events

Midwife

B

A → This infill development project in Berlin, architecturally attractive but also challenging, unites today's timber construction options with current demands for developing communities.

B → The diversity of uses in c13 reunites the existential functions – living, working, leisure, education, and culture – that had become separated in the 20th century.

C → Moving the new building clear of the neighbouring fire wall in some places has resulted in additional lightwells and outdoor seating areas instead of the customary totally closed side to the building.

141

C

in mind. The building of c13 enabled the foundation to use architecture to demonstrate a view of sustainability that matches the foundation's own values. With owner-occupied and rented apartments, offices, an apartment shared by students, child daycare amenity, midwifery and paediatric surgery, physiotherapy / occupational therapy centre, painting studio, the 'Kiezküche' café, a seminar and event centre that can be hired out, family counselling centre and so on, the multifunctionality of the building's usage turns it into the nucleus of a new neighbourhood.

Small town in the big city

As the architect Tom Kaden explains, the small town in the big city revives the spirit of rediscovered solidarity and intermeshing of existential functions through a vertical and horizontal mix. Everything is compact, diversity has a capital D, the occupants are socially committed, and caring is important again. The foundation's principle is holistic and understood as both a socio-economic and socio-political signal that is intended to leave a permanent mark on this neighbourhood. With their integrated architecture and planning approach, Kaden und Partner have assisted the creation of a new community and hence taken a stand against advancing gentrification in whole city districts. Also in Prenzlauer Berg, where a great deal of the former diversity in terms of age structures, biographies, lifestyles, and jobs has already given way to monetary dullness and social monotony. It is now up to the people to unite the separate functions and integrate them into a new social, urban context of diversity that must be established. mwl

Client **Stiftung für Bildung.Werte.Leben, 10405 Berlin, Germany, www.bildung-werte-leben.de**

Architecture / Site supervision **Kaden und Partner Architekten, 10178 Berlin, Germany, www.kadenundlager.de**

General contractor, timber **oa.sys baut GmbH, 6861 Alberschwende, Austria, www.oa-sys.com**

Structural engineering, timber **Pirmin Jung Ingenieure für Holzbau AG, 6026 Rain, Switzerland, www.pirminjung.ch**

Building services (design & site supervision) **Planungsbüro Roth, 15344 Strausberg, Germany, www.pb-roth.de**

Electrical engineers **Planungsbüro Marion Fabis, 14532 Kleinmachnow, Germany, www.pb-fabis.de**

Fire protection **Dehne, Kruse Brandschutzingenieure GmbH & Co. KG, 38518 Gifhorn, Germany, www.kd-brandschutz.de**

Gross floor area **2820 m²**

Net developed area **2514 m²**

Usable floor area, commercial **1640 m²**

Usable floor area, residential **930 m²**

Area of plot **900 m²**

Site occupancy index **0.63**

Plot ratio **3.1**

Transmission heat losses during heating period QT **9597 kWh/a**

Ventilation heat losses during heating period QV **1578 kWh/a**

Internal heat gains during heating period Qi **3936 kWh/a**

Passive solar heat gains during heating period Qs **6496 kWh/a**

Primary energy requirement (actual building value) **358.1 kWh (m²a)**

Building costs, groups 3 + 4, net **approx. €1550/m² residential floor area**

Building costs, total **€7 million**

Quantity of timber used **600 m³**

Carbon (C) content **150 t**

Sequestered CO₂ **550 t**

A → This timber building with its healthy interior climate makes skilful use of light and transparency.

B → The relationship between the timber parts (brown) and the concrete parts (grey) shows how and where timber can achieve much more efficient use of resources in construction.

C → A grid of steel beams on timber columns covers the full 45 metre depth of the building.

A

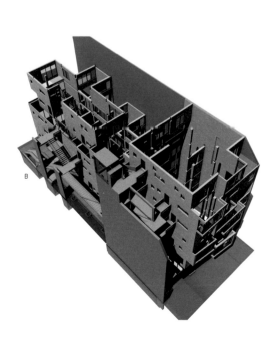

B

C

Europe's biggest additional storey project in timber

An extra storey has been added to a former production and office building in Nuremberg. This huge task – the floor area was bigger than a football pitch – was completed in just five months thanks to modern timber construction.

During the 1970s the Quelle Group expanded its operations by building two production buildings and an office wing, with a total floor area of about 25 000 m², in the southern part of Nuremberg. Business was flourishing for Foto Quelle and so the mail-order group ensured that the structural design of the industrial complex, equipped with one of the most modern and largest photo laboratories in Europe, could cope with up to three additional storeys. But it wasn't to be. The bottom dropped out of the analogue photography market. Following a period when the complex stood empty, it was then bought by a property developer. The former brownfield site has been modernised, converted, and extended upwards in three construction phases. The abbreviation TM50 (Thomas-Mann-Straße 50) now stands for the successful conversion of a former commercial site. It has been turned into a modern service and administration centre with attractive office and production facilities, retailing, and restaurants employing contemporary architecture.

Vertical infill developments in growing conurbations
Although population figures are stagnating, even declining, conurbations are growing incessantly. Land for building in urban areas is becoming scarcer and more expensive. Research and discussions among experts have come to the conclusion that besides the general increase in the density of development, infill developments, i.e. building on sites already developed, is just as realistic as it is desirable from the urban planning viewpoint. Infill developments do not require precious building plots in order to erect the buildings so urgently needed for homes and businesses, but instead tend to increase the value of the existing building stock, which is often refurbished at the same time. Besides, identifying new areas for development is expensive and the numerous constraints, e.g. retaining open areas and clearances to existing buildings, seriously restrict the options. Further, it is also important to stop uncontrolled (sub)urban sprawl and ground sealing. On top of that, with higher densities, more companies and more people can use the expensive transport and services infrastructures, which in the end results in a lower consumption of energy and resources per head of population. In addition, high-density developments result in lower follow-up costs for the upkeep of infrastructure elements than is the case with low-density structures. Finally, the areas of greenery so crucial for a high quality of life remain intact.

Prefabrication and fast progress on site
In the sensitive surroundings of high-density city districts and commercial zones, building sites represent a major challenge for businesses, residents, and building contractors alike. All those involved should be integrated into the planned construction project at an early stage in order to prevent disruptions and delays during construction. Another factor that needs to be taken into account is rent rebates, which have to be added to the building costs if the construction work is considered to constitute an unreasonable nuisance. Therefore, reducing the construction phase to a minimum is of prime importance. Computer-controlled, fully automatic CNC machining results in highly accurate factory-produced timber elements. The high degree of prefabrication, with virtually

Harmony between all aspects of design and construction is typical of a 21st century timber architecture that integrates the existing concrete structure and at the same time produces a self-confident, distinct architectural vocabulary.

all components delivered to site just in time and complete with insulation, channels for pipes and cables plus door and window openings, ensures that work on site is less dependent on the weather and that realistic timetables can be drawn up. Although modern engineered timber construction requires more elaborate planning, it still requires only about half the time on site compared with conventional forms of construction.

Another advantage is that adding more storeys in timber involves comparatively low levels of dust and noise. The components are positioned exactly with a crane and fixed immediately. The rapid progress on site is quite obvious to others, too, which increases the acceptance and tolerance among the local population. Along with this there is the fact that the extra storey can be used as efficiently as possible in order to create the maximum floor area. By incorporating the insulating layer in the load-bearing layer, it is possible to design thinner wall cross-sections with the same insulation value than would be the case with purely mineral forms of construction. That means larger lettable units can be realised on the same plan area. Furthermore, the weight advantage of extra storeys and extensions in lightweight timber construction can be exploited because the loads on the existing load-bearing structure are lower than would be the case for designs using much heavier steel, concrete, or masonry, which in turn minimises the costs.

Extension with building still in use

The challenge for the timber contractor, HU-Holzunion, was to add the third floor as smoothly and quickly as possible, because the companies on the lower floors had to be able to continue working undisturbed. This monumental extra storey project in timber, with a plan area of about 5000 m², was completed in just five months, from early October 2014 to late February 2015. Owing to the size of this additional storey, 74 × 102 metres, HU-Holzunion, a joint venture between several independent timber contractors set up specially for such large construction projects, has effectively proved that timber construction, which is characterised by small and mid-size businesses, can also play a vital role in large-scale building projects when skills are amalgamated. This consortium of four (now five) timber contractors made it possible to develop the diverse separate elements in large batches simultaneously at several locations and deliver them on time and ready to erect. The project included about 80 trusses 11.80 metres long (connected with punched metal-plate fasteners), 80 floor elements measuring 2.60 × 11.70 metres and 180 roof elements with a maximum size of 3 × 12.50 metres.

Complex big site management

This project comprised the energy-efficiency upgrade of the mineral building envelope to the ground and first floors using suspended timber elements, mostly finished with a mineral render facade, plus the construction of an additional storey using a timber frame and cross-laminated timber (CLT). In some places the new storey has a ceiling height of 7 metres and so includes a mezzanine floor. Whereas the Taglieber company was responsible for prefabricating the timber-frame walls, including integral wood/aluminium windows, Cordes Holzbau provided the glued laminated timber columns and the trusses with their rigid corner connections as well as the floor and roof elements. The CLT elements for the double towers were prefabricated by Stora Enso, and the Karl Hoffmeister carpentry shop measured up the Eternit facades (relevant for fire protection) on site, cut them to size in the shop with a special saw, and then erected them on site. The coordination of the diverse tasks called for a strict site management normally called for on big sites in order to guarantee functioning site logistics right up to the delivery of the prefabricated elements in accordance with the timetable.

Striking roof form and lightwells

The eastern part of the additional storey consists of five blocks. These are positioned offset, with the projecting segments extending the five existing double towers with stairs and lifts on the north and south sides of the building. The ends of the blocks are distinctive and appear to be monopitch roofs at first sight. However, closer inspection reveals them to be very shallow duo-pitch roofs with their eaves above the double towers. From there, each roof continues down the double tower facade – looking like a set of five clamps over the building. On the eastern block the roof continues down the facade, then – in the form of a horizontal canopy at half height – meanders two-thirds of the way along the east side before dropping vertically to the ground. This stylistic element guides visitors to the main entrance. Between the five pitched roofs on the blocks there are eight lower interconnecting sections with flat roofs. The five main blocks and these eight lower sections surround four spacious internal courtyards that allow daylight to reach 55 metres deep into the building. Parts of the old precast concrete floors were removed for this purpose.

The roof ridges mark the points where the double towers begin. The positions of the double towers alternate between the north (three towers) and south (two towers) elevations. This asymmetry and the offset blocks ensure an eye-catching appearance for the

A → The section illustrates the structure of the TM50 with its five raised blocks and four intervening courtyards.

B → The plan of the 2nd floor shows the grid and the magnitude of the additional storeys, which were finished with a mineral render facade on a wood fibre insulating board background.

C → The internal courtyards 'chiselled out' of the concrete building allow daylight to reach the interior of the voluminous TM50 so that offices can be positioned where otherwise only dark storage areas would have been possible.

D → The large conference room for the Federal Employment Agency demonstrates timber construction by way of exposed glulam columns, the acoustic ceiling lined in silver fir, and the CLT wall in spruce.

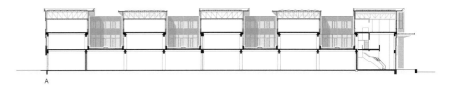

A

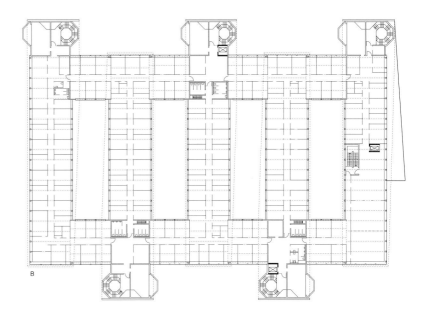

B

147

C

D

TM50, whose shallow pitched roofs comprise a kind of fifth facade to round off the complex. The sculpted roof form, finished with grey synthetic waterproofing (roof surfaces) and black EPDM foil (vertical signboards), brings this industrial utility building of the 1970s into the 21st century with its flexible services and modern information technologies. The timber refurbishment and additional storey break up the originally rigid form of the building without denying its origins. The transition from the secondary to the tertiary and quaternary sectors of the economy takes place smoothly. The new has been built on the old, the timber top on the mineral base. The architecture, materials, and concept of the TM50 reflect the social changes in the nature of employment and the changes in building culture; the pure pragmatism of the past, expressed in mineral form, contrasting with timber's efficient use of resources, load-carrying capacity, and beauty. This is visible at several places: on the walls to the internal courtyards (in the form of vertical larch cladding), on the parapets between the blocks (rhombus-shaped larch battens), and on the soffits to the roof overhangs (larch three-ply core plywood).

Trusses supported on glulam columns

The three apparently identical middle blocks had to accommodate the differences in the mineral substructure, partly due to isolating joints across the building. Therefore, the sizes of the individual elements and the glulam trusses are different for each of these three blocks. The tapering roof overhang is not exactly the same size, either.

The roofs to the double towers are made of a CLT assembly with insulation above the rafters. The roof overhangs, up to 2.50 metres long, are made of prefabricated cantilevering purlin elements that are screwed to a CLT frame. On the underside they are clad with cross-banded three-ply core plywood and on the top there is a sheathing of tongue and groove boards. The unitised, load-bearing roof structure traces the existing 10.80 metre grid and consists of trusses (connected with punched metal-plate fasteners) with different depths at a spacing of 2.70 metres which are supported on glulam columns. The trusses and columns have connection details that create a rigid frame and thus guarantee the building's stability in the transverse direction. In addition, the posts connect to the timber-frame walls, which terminate at the underside of the trusses. The gables, which contribute to the stability of the building and are assembled from 'cold-wall' (= with ventilation cavity) elements, are supported on these. The suspended floor elements (solid structural timber joists with exposed OSB soffit and filled with blown cellulose insulation) are supported on the bottom chords of the trusses, which have laminated veneer lumber (LVL) nibs on both sides for this purpose. The roof elements (in the form of hinged purlins every 83 centimetres, with tongue and groove boards on top and three-ply core plywood soffits to the roof overhang) were likewise prefabricated and are laid on top of the trusses. With the additional storey, the height to the eaves is 14.95 metres, and the highest point on the gables is 16.60 metres above the ground.

Geothermal, zero-emissions energy supply

The heating and cooling systems in the TM50 building achieve zero emissions on the basis of shallow geothermal energy. An array of borehole heat exchangers (BHEs) about 100 metres deep has been installed on a grid. The dual-circuit thermoactive components connected to these heat the building in winter and cool it in summer. Heat is extracted from the ground via the BHEs in the winter, which cools the ground at the same time. This cooling effect is exploited in the following summer, when heat from the building flows back into the ground ready for the next winter. This self-recharging, seasonal energy storage concept covers the base heating/cooling load for the TM50 over the whole year.

Whereas on the existing floors the energy was supplied via underfloor heating and radiant ceiling panels, only the latter is required in the new storey. mwl

A → The five blocks with their intervening lightwells reflect the process of change from rational block architecture to a more open architectural language.

B → Competitive advantages through a consortium of small and mid-size businesses: prefabrication of large batches on time thanks to parallel production at several locations

C → Adding a storey also means that the energy and raw materials embodied in the existing, mineral building can be used for further decades with the help of timber.

D → The load-bearing structure for the additional storey was erected with maximum precision and maximum speed.

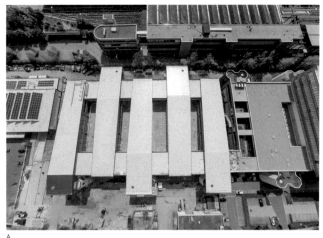

A

B

Client BGB Gesellschaft Helmut Schmelzer GmbH, Nuremberg, Germany, www.tm50.de

Architecture DXV Architektur, Nuremberg, Germany, www.dxv-architektur.com

Project management Projektsteuerung Häberlein, Feuchtwangen, Germany, www.projektsteuerung-haeberlein.de

Timber contractor HU-Holzunion GmbH, Rotenburg (Wümme)/Oettingen, Germany, www.holzunion.com

Structural engineering, carcass Trafektum GbR, Nuremberg, Germany, www.trafektum.de

Structural engineering, timber Häussler Ingenieure GmbH, Kempten, Germany, www.haeussler-ingenieure.com

Fire protection Ulm Ingenieurgesellschaft , Erlangen, Germany, www.ulm-ig.org

Quantity surveyor Vermessungsbüro Robert Ziegler, Nuremberg, Germany, www.vermziegler.de

Building services Ingenieurteam Plansache GmbH, Nuremberg, Germany, www.it-plansache.de

Thermal insulation Werkhaus Architekten, Nuremberg, Germany

Building physics Wolfgang Sorge Ingenieurbüro, Nuremberg, Germany, www.ifbsorge.de

Geothermal consultant CDM Smith Consult GmbH, Nuremberg, Germany, www.cdmsmith.com

Floor area 15 800 m²

Volume of building 75 000 m³

Primary usable floor area, new & converted areas (1st & 2nd floors / offices) 5200 m²

Primary usable floor area, existing (ground floor / commercial) 1850 m²

Area covered by building 6400 m²

External areas 4600 m²

Building category building regulations class 5

Annual primary energy requirement 106.18 kWh (m²a)

Transmission heat losses 0.486 W/m²K

Start on site (structural carcass / demolition) April 2014

Start on site (timber construction) October 2014

Completion (timber) February 2015

Final completion August 2015

Costs €16 million

Quantity of timber used 1550 m³

Carbon (C) content 387 t

CO_2 sequestration 1420 t

C

D

Special structures

Solid timber cross-in-square church

Wooden churches are usually relics of the distant past. In the Rhön Mountains, however, an industrially prefabricated, unitised form of timber construction has been used to build a new church for the Skete of St Spyridon, a community of Serbian Orthodox monks.

This wooden church serves as a spiritual centre for a monastery designed as a self-sufficient hermitage. In the light of the growing numbers of monks, pilgrims, and others visiting the skete, especially on Sundays and feast days, the client, the Serbian Orthodox Church, was unable to offer them all enough space. The new rural location, previously the site of an old mill, was chosen intentionally to take up the reference to nature and extend it to the timber church structure, surrounded by meadows with old fruit trees, as a quiet place for contemplative reflection. The church, which was funded entirely from donations, forms the centre of the community of monks. It is modelled on the historic monastic church at Gradac in Serbia, which dates from the late 13th century. Nevertheless, it differs fundamentally from that stone structure in that the new church has been built in solid timber over a reinforced concrete basement (which contains rooms for the heating plant and sanitary facilities). Furthermore, the design and decoration also include elements of Romanesque sacred buildings. The architect Norman Heimbrodt masterminded the development of the concept, likewise the detailed design and construction. He introduced the Serbian Orthodox Church to the idea of using solid timber, which was unusual to them, studied the original in Serbia and implemented the knowledge gained there together with the carpenters and timber design engineers from contractor Herrmann Massivholzhaus.

Industrial production

The industrially manufactured MHM solid timber wall system was used for this church. The invention is based on the many years of experience of a Bavarian manufacturer of precision machinery for the international woodworking industry. Owing to the company's excellent insight into the sawmill sector, they recognised that the less-sought-after side boards resulting from the conversion process could be used to produce industrially prefabricated solid timber modules and hence solid timber buildings. Further development of existing woodworking machinery enabled simple softwood boards obtained locally to be turned into complete wall elements in serial production on semi-automatic production lines – and without the use of chemical additives or adhesives. First, the timber is dried to a residual moisture content of about 15 per cent, which makes it dimensionally stable and resistant to pests. The next step involves cutting grooves in the boards during planing to a constant thickness of 23 millimetres. In the final wall system, the grooves retain air, which improves the already excellent insulating properties of the solid timber even further without increasing its weight or volume.

Stationary layer of air

Next, the layers of boards are pressed together in a cross-banded lay-up. Small, diagonal aluminium pins fasten the individual layers together, which ensures high strength within each system element. Assembling the wall panels in this way rules out any subsequent settlement,

The design of the ecclesiastical timber architecture was based on the traditions of old master-builders in accordance with the golden section principle.

swelling, and shrinkage of the wood. Finally, the computer-controlled plant cuts the solid timber components to size with millimetre precision, also cutting openings for doors and windows and channels for pipes and cables.

Despite the industrial prefabrication, all the advantages of solid timber forms of construction, the building ecology, environmental hygiene, and interior climate, for instance, are retained. The modules are diffusion-permeable, dry, stable, and load-bearing; they exhibit good sorption, heat storage, and thermal insulation properties, and they consume little energy during production.

As a final operation, a mortar mix made from wax, sunflower oil, and sawdust is spread over the ends and joints of the solid timber elements. The mortar protects the wall components against moisture and seals off the grooves, which guarantees the stationary layer of air needed to optimise the thermal insulation. The MHM system thus achieves a thermal conductivity of 0.0943 W/mK, whereas pure softwood without a stationary layer of air only manages a value of 0.13 W/mK.

Wood fibre insulating board as background for render

Owing to its monolithic, precise, solid timber composition, the industrial production system offers above-average sound insulation and fire protection. In addition, the diffusion-permeable, single-material nature of the building also prevents heat losses due to thermal bridges. Further advantages of the computer-controlled production are the accuracy of fit and the time-savings. From the ground slab upwards, the construction, including the roof structure, could be carried out exactly as planned. The elements were lifted into place with a crane and immediately screwed together. It took only fourteen working days to erect the structural carcass for the church. All load-bearing internal and external walls for the church are made of 34 centimetre thick MHM elements (only the partitions in the small caretaker's flat are 11.5 centimetres thick). This is the maximum thickness feasible with the MHM system. The fifteen layers of boards have a theoretical U-value of 0.239 W/m²K and do not require any additional insulation. The 10 centimetre thick wood fibre insulating boards attached on the outside function as a background for the render, which increases the visual mass of the walls. A mineral render system was then applied, making the external walls almost 50 centimetres thick. The layer of wood fibre insulation boards constitutes extra insulation, so the church has a highly insulating, compact building envelope. Inside the church, the wooden surfaces were left exposed only temporarily. In keeping with Orthodox traditions, historic frescoes were painted on the walls, applied directly to a multi-coat lime plaster (on a mineral board background) while it was still wet.

A cruciform ground plan

The architecture of the solid timber church is governed by the central square *naos,* the equivalent of the crossing in traditional Western church architecture, which boasts an area of 64 m². The plan form of the single-nave church is that of a cross, with the nave being longer than the chancel and the transepts being lower and smaller in area. The underlying principle here is the style of Byzantine churches, which has characterised the buildings of the Orthodox Church since the 9th century. Four smaller areas aligned with the main points of the compass join up with the crossing, where nave and transept meet. The chancel with the three apses behind faces east. The crossing is roofed over by a large 5.2 tonne dome, the top of which is 14.60 metres above floor level. It is this dome that gives the church its distinctive external appearance and is also responsible for the name of this type of ecclesiastical structure – the cross-in-square church. The apparently round dome is based on an octagon on top of an ellipsis. In this arrangement only two surfaces make contact with an imaginary circle, while the other surfaces form the elliptical opening, which presented the timber contractor with a construction challenge. The dome is made up of thirty-two curved glued laminated timber ribs and four three-pin frames. The crossing is in turn bordered and supported by two large round arches in glued laminated timber, whereas the two smaller arches are made from MHM elements. Standing seam zinc sheets have been used for the roof finish to the dome. Each zinc sheet was turned up along the sides and placed directly alongside the next one. The bent-up edges were joined with a single fold.

Golden section – union of symmetry and asymmetry

Round windows and also large arches (up to a maximum dimension governed by the machinery) can be cut in MHM system elements. One of the factors limiting the size is the maximum panel dimensions that can be machined (3 × 6 m).

The construction of this church required an efficient correlation between the structural requirements and the prefabrication options available for the timber elements. One outcome of that was the use of 24 millimetre thick plywood strips let into the timber at the joints to ensure the longitudinal stability of the central nave. The three apses are made of several mitre-cut solid timber elements that together create a semicircle. Likewise, their dome-like lean-to roofs are made up of many small flat segments formed by hip rafters and 28 millimetre thick tongue and groove sheathing. The round arch windows in the apses could not be fabricated completely on the MHM machines because they extend over three elements. A small part of each window therefore had to be cut manually.

A

B

A → The solid timber Serbian Orthodox Church is built on a gentle slope over a reinforced concrete basement.

B → The CAD-assisted design and factory-prefabrication of modern engineered timber construction mean that operations that in the past required many hours of manual work can now be carried out in a short time with maximum precision.

In his design for this cross-in-square church, architect Norman Heimbrodt adhered to the proportions of the 'golden section'. This design principle known since ancient times can be understood as integrity in disparity. It is not about the symmetry of the individual parts within the framework of a dualistic observation. The dimensions are related in that the ratio between the smaller component and the larger one is exactly the same as that between the larger component and the whole. Symmetry is not achieved on the singular level of the equivalence of the individual parts and forms, but on the level of the unity and equivalence of the proportions.

Departing from the dictates of the right angle

Underlying this principle is the knowledge that overall symmetry is able to integrate individual asymmetries.

The credibility of individual components that are asymmetric with other individual components is confirmed by considering the success of the church's architecture as a whole. Only the whole is consummate, and this ratio of proportions is perceived by human beings as harmonious and coherent. Therefore, the side aisles of the church are partly asymmetric about the dome, likewise some wall/floor junctions, which the carpenter constructed with rising wall plates, are not at an angle of 90°. Furthermore, the nave is not exactly in line with the axis of the crossing, which means that the main axis of the church is at a slight angle. Departing from the dictates of the right angle, a device employed by the master-builders of the past, too, introduces a subtle movement into the church which is reflected in a play of light and grandeur. mwl

A

B

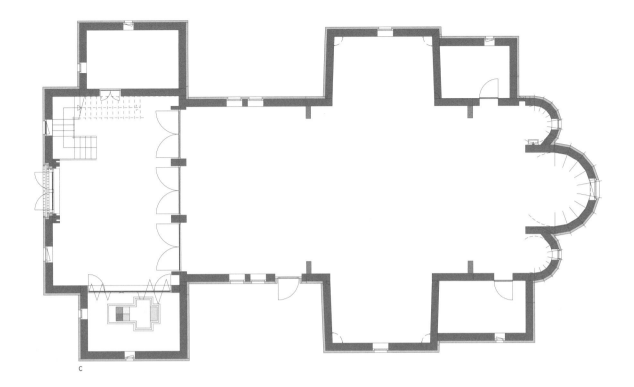

C

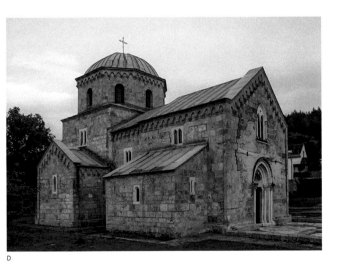

D

A → The timber structural carcass to the cross-in-square church, which is finished with a mineral render, was erected in just fourteen days.

B → Good to know: the grooved layers of boards sealed with a special mortar mix trap a layer of stationary air within the component, which increases the insulating effect of each MHM element.

C → The plan form of the single-nave church is that of a cross, with the nave being longer than the chancel and the transepts being lower and smaller in area.

D → The 'prototype': the single-nave monastic church at Gradac in Serbia, built around 1270, is based on Byzantine architecture and decorated with Romanesque and Gothic elements.

Client Gesellschaft zur Förderung der orthodoxen Spiritualität e.V. (GFOS e.V. Geilnau), Eiterfeld-Unterufhausen, Germany, www.spyridon-skite.de

Architecture Norman Heimbrodt Architekt, Hünfeld, Germany, www.heimbrodt.com

Timber contractor Herrmann Massivholzhaus GmbH, Geisa, Germany, www.herrmann-massivholzhaus.de

Glulam round arches W.u.J.Derix GmbH & Co., Niederkrüchten, Germany; Poppensieker & Derix GmbH & Co. KG, Westerkappeln, Germany, www.derix.de

Structural calculations / Load-bearing structure Basement: Dipl.-Ing.Jürgen Held, Hünfeld, Germany; Timber structure: Dipl.-Ing.Christian Heil, Künzell, Germany, www.heil-bsb.de

Reinforced concrete basement Aventa-Nord GmbH, Sittensen, Germany, www.aventa-nord.de

Church windows Schreinerei Hartmut Both, Tann, Germany, www.both-wintergarten.de

Render Ampora Wärmedämmung GmbH, Darmstadt, Germany

Usable floor area 532 m²

Enclosed volume 2766 m³

Costs, basement + timber structural carcass €600 000

Quantity of timber used 300 m³

Carbon (C) content 75 t

CO_2 sequestration 275 t

New farmyard evokes old covered market traditions

The innovative farmyard design of Overmeyer organic farm in Seevetal south of Hamburg is a new highlight among the communities in the flat countryside. The diversity of the materials and design has resulted in a successful symbiosis of ecological timber construction and organic agriculture.

Throughout Europe, farms being abandoned or turned into housing have been the general trend for many decades. Building completely new farms, and in undeveloped areas, too, has never figured on the agenda – until now. The client, a married couple, had been successfully running an organic farm and shop under a lease agreement since 1995. However, rebuilding was the only way of dealing fully with the different needs and demands of contemporary organic farming operations, including on-farm processing and direct marketing. With twenty-one permanent staff and thirteen others on so-called mini-job contracts, it was the economic importance of this farm for this rural region that helped to secure approval for a construction project in an undeveloped area through a change in the land-use plan.

Village-type character
The farmers themselves organised an architectural competition, which led to an urban/open land concept that is based on the rural, four-sided farmyard style seen widely throughout Central Europe. In this historic farmyard form, the farmhouse and outbuildings are all separate structures arranged opposite each other around a large open area; they create a kind of self-sufficient little village.

An open form was chosen for this organic farm to increase the appeal for visitors – several hundred every day. In addition, the arrangement of the various buildings on this greenfield site should create a distinct settlement-type character counteracting the sense of being lost in the broad landscape. To prevent this framework from appearing too rigid, the buildings were not placed at exactly 90 degrees to each other, as was usual with such farms in the past. All four buildings – farmhouse, market hall with shop and on-farm processing, barn, stables, and henhouses – are reached from the central yard. The balance between proximity and open space is successful. With all the agricultural buildings in sight, they fuse together again what the subdivision of work in modern businesses has torn apart: living, working, leisure, production, on-farm processing and direct sales to consumers, and, of course, self-sufficiency.

Building without disturbing farm operations
The whole complex has been built with modern prefabricated timber-frame and timber-panel elements, which were ready supplied with facade sheathing and different external cladding solutions. Being not far away, the Hamburg-based architectural practice Scaven Hütz was appointed to take charge of design and site supervision. Although BeL Sozietät für Architektur in Cologne

The farmyard draws its animated character from the interplay of materials and surfaces, form, and design.

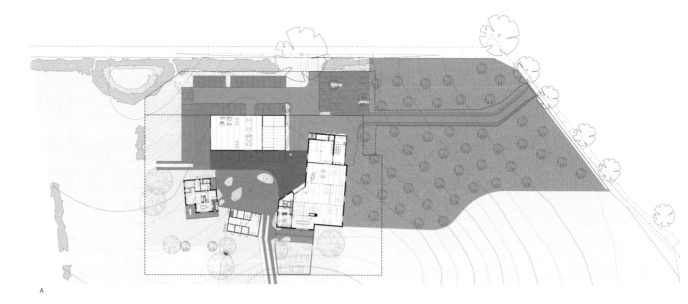

A

B

C

D

A → True to the historical farmyard form, the farmhouse and outbuildings are grouped around a large open area that serves as a central 'distribution' zone and as a place to meet and talk.

B → The successful interaction between design concept and landscape architecture formed the foundation for the highly diverse yet stylish realisation of this organic farm.

C → The farm shop revives the spirit of old covered markets and exploits transparency to show what it has to offer.

D → Readily visible here is the timber and steel load-bearing structure to the three-bay shop and on-farm processing area.

E+F → The village-type character of the four-sided farmyard blends harmoniously into the flat landscape. The buildings are not at 90° to each other, which helps integration into the mature, scattered structure of the farms of this region.

G → The central farmyard surrounded by farmhouse, barn, stables, henhouses, and shop blends seamlessly into the surrounding landscape of fields and reveals the direct connection with organic agriculture.

E

F

G

was responsible for producing drawings for approval and also some of the fabrication drawings, most of the working drawings were produced by Scaven Hütz, with the architects also introducing new elements into the internal and external design. Time was a crucial factor for the client when choosing the type of timber construction, as the new buildings had to be integrated without disturbing daily farming operations. Wood, as a renewable material, was a favourite with the organic farmers anyway. What also convinced them was the fact that the high degree of prefabrication in the individual timber components enabled construction phases to be planned exactly, with a total construction time that could be realistically calculated. It is the heterogeneous appearance of the group of buildings, distinguished by their different surface finishes, that impresses the observer.

Interplay of facades and surfaces

Timber facades in various forms have been combined with facing brickwork that integrates local building traditions and at the same time makes a subtle contrast with the wooden surfaces. The interplay between the horizontal and vertical timber finishes generates an organic vitality that reflects its fertile agriculture origins. At the farmhouse, the cladding is in the form of horizontal rhombus-shaped battens made of weather-resistant Siberian larch in various thicknesses. The farm shop, however, has rhombus-shaped battens made of European larch, and the storerooms directly alongside are different again, with two different types of larch facade: ranch-style shiplap boarding made of waney-edged, debarked planks, whose rough texture is not the only thing that gives this finish a Wild West look, and, around the cold store, vertical, sawn boards in different widths which were attached with gaps and maintain the reference to nature and the native soil. This diversity continues in the roof covering. Whereas the two-storey shop/office wing is finished with reddish brown clay roof tiles, the storeroom has a monopitch green roof planted with essentially natural forms of vegetation and the shop for organic produce has a roof of metal trapezoidal profile sheets. And the farmhouse has both – clay tiles and green roof. These variations lend the small village character of the organic farm a constant dynamic impulse that encourages and reflects the natural change of things. Development has been understood for what it is: a constant process. Architecture and agriculture speak one and the same language here.

Cellular glass granulate and cellulose insulation

None of the buildings has a basement and so the ground floor slabs were founded on a load-bearing layer of recycled cellular glass granulate. This relatively lightweight, ageing-resistant material insulates the buildings against the soil without any thermal bridges, and also provides a drainage function. The timber frames for the farmyard buildings are made of solid structural timber sections and, like the roof elements, are insulated with an ecological, blown insulation made of recycled cellulose fibres. The stability of the external frames is ensured by 15 millimetre OSB (external wall) or 25 millimetre OSB (shop roof) sheathing on the inside. The organic farmyard complies with fire resistance class F30. To achieve this, steel components were coated with an intumescent paint. The walls (U-value = 0.17 W/m²K) made of timber-frame elements comply with the fire resistance requirements by using the following construction: 15 millimetre OSB and gypsum fire-resistant boards (GKF) on the inside, followed by insulated, 24 centimetre thick studs and rails finished on the outside with an 18 millimetre thick wood fibre insulating board. The soffits of the roof elements are made of 25 millimetre thick OSB and are left exposed, whereas 15 millimetre thick MDF boards are used on top. Only the internal wall of the storeroom had to meet F90-B fire resistance requirements, which was achieved with a double layer of 15 millimetre gypsum fibreboard on both sides.

Load-bearing structures in timber and steel

The heart of this vegetable farm, the 500 m² shop for organic produce, with its adjacent area for on-farm processing, the 'living room' with fireplace, sofas, dining tables, and a panoramic view over the fields, storerooms, and cold store, reminds the observer of the traditions of old covered markets. Each of the three bays making up the pitched roof to this mixed-use building spans 8.75 metres and has a roof pitch of 30 degrees. The primary structure has been left exposed. It consists of trussed steel rafters supported on steel circular hollow section columns internally and reinforced concrete columns incorporated into the external timber-frame walls. The concrete columns are also responsible for the building's stability. Along the wall separating the shop from the storerooms, the steel trusses are supported on timber columns within the timber wall. The simply supported purlin roof elements are connected to the steel trusses via timber plates bolted to the trusses.

On the ground floor there is the shop, a plant room, storerooms, the on-farm processing area, and a WC for customers. The upper floor, with offices and staff amenities, is formed by a structure of glued laminated timber beams, which are left exposed and supported on and braced by two reinforced concrete columns in the shop below. Contrasting with this, the ground and suspended floors to the two-part, two-storey barn were built in reinforced concrete, whereas the upper floor and walls to the timber-frame building are exposed, carpentry-style assemblies. The compact house for the client's family is not unlike a North American farmhouse. The south side has a porch that, with the roof overhanging a generous 2 metres, provides an outdoor seating area that can be used regardless of the weather.

Heat from the refrigeration system
The space heating and hot water systems for the building are based on a multi-stage concept. The base load is covered by recovering waste heat from the refrigeration system, which runs all year round. There are 20 metres of multi-deck display chillers and refrigerated counters in the shop, a 2 metre long cold counter for the on-farm processing plus three cold stores. Together, they supply the necessary heat energy. A heat exchanger extracts this energy from the condenser and feeds it to two interim storage units, each with a capacity of 1500 litres. From there the energy is fed to the underfloor heating systems in the house, the shop, and the on-farm processing area. Such heating systems require only a low flow temperature of 30 to 35°C. Only the office area has individually controlled radiators. In addition, in the house, the internal walls of which are finished with an ecological, natural loam plaster in some places, there is a central wood-fired stove with an output of 6 kW which can also be used for cooking and baking. A gas-fired condensing boiler is available as a backup and to cover peak loads in the winter. mwl

A

B

A → The farmhouse is clad in horizontal rhombus-shaped battens made from weather-resistant Siberian larch in various thicknesses of 27 to 40 millimetres. They were attached with gaps of up to 10 millimetres which emphasise the organic timber construction.

B → What was once thought of as a model on the way out returns here in the form of a high-quality, striking timber design: a family farm with a real identity which attracts people who care about what they buy.

Client Overmeyer GbR, 21218 Seevetal OT Emmelndorf, Germany, www.overmeyer-landbaukultur.de

Architecture, HOAI service phases I–IV BeL Sozietät für Architektur BDA, 50672 Cologne, Germany, www.bel.cx

Architecture, HOAI service phases V–IX Scaven Hütz Architekt, 21079 Hamburg, Germany, www.scavenhuetz.de

Timber contractor for shop, on-farm processing area, storerooms, barn Holzbau Cordes, 21079 Hamburg, Germany, www.cordes-holzbau.de

Timber contractor for house, stables Meisterkollektiv, 21224 Rosengarten, Germany, www.meister-kollektiv.de

Structural engineering, HOAI service phases I–IV Ingenieurbüro Jürgen Bernhardt, 50668 Cologne, Germany

Structural engineering, calculations: Dr Möller & Oberhokamp Beratende Ingenieure im Bauwesen, 32657; Lemgo, Germany, www.statik-owl.de

Urban planning concept & landscape architecture Urban Catalyst Studio, 12435 Berlin, Germany, www.urbancatalyst-studio.de; BeL Sozietät für Architektur BDA, 50672 Cologne, Germany

Strategic development Günther van Ravenzwaay, 21218 Seevetal, Germany; Urban Catalyst Studio, 12435 Berlin, Germany

Interior architecture, shop Architekturpraxis Anja Herold, 12159 Berlin, Germany, www.architekturpraxis.com

House 290 m²

Barn 465 m²

Stables + henhouses 185 m²

Shop 513 m²

Costs €3.5 million

Quantity of timber used 207 m³

Carbon (C) content 52 t

Sequestered CO_2 190 t

Viewing tower on the Pyramidenkogel

Since June 2013 there has been a 100 metre high viewing tower overlooking the Wörthersee, a lake in Carinthia, Austria. The tower on top of the Pyramidenkogel has a load-bearing structure of steel and timber and is currently the tallest of its kind in the world. Although its geometry is based on just four numbers, the design and fabrication of the members still needed considerable creative skill besides engineering expertise.

Until it was demolished in October 2012, a 54 metre high reinforced concrete viewing and broadcasting tower, built in 1968, occupied the site. Construction of the new tower took only eight months, which meant Keutschach local authority could open their new tourist attraction in June 2013. Difficult ownership issues, changing circumstances for tourism and the poor state of the old tower led to the decision to replace it. The desire for a contemporary, innovative solution was a priority of the architectural competition organised in 2007. The competition rules also stipulated the use of timber – an indigenous, ecologically sustainable, and at the same time innovative building material. Furthermore, the architectural design of the tower had to be unique and satisfy the latest demands for tourist attractions.

The vision: an accessible sculpture

Right from the start, the team that eventually won the competition wanted to create an accessible sculpture open on all sides. It had to be interesting to look at from all directions, but the design should not be based on a circle. The idea of a geometrically generated envelope based on an elliptical plan proved to be the right approach. The result is a sculpture that winds itself skywards, offset about its centre by a certain dimension each time, creating an organic, seemingly almost feminine form.

The tower structure that grew from this basic idea consists of sixteen single-curvature columns made of larch glued laminated timber. The column bases are set out radially on an elliptical plan, their axes pointing towards the centre of the tower. Ten elliptical steel rings, which are rotated clockwise through 22.5 degrees every

Together with the antenna, the new viewing tower – a graceful steel-and-timber structure – is 100 metres high. The highest viewing platform is at 70.40 metres. From here, visitors can enjoy a breathtaking view of Carinthia's lakes and mountains.

6.40 metres vertically, and eighty diagonal braces stabilise the helical structure as it rises from the ground.

This project called for close collaboration between the architects and the structural engineers. During the various steps of the preliminary design, the construction considerations and the geometrical requirements were gradually harmonised so that a series of identical members in a structured global arrangement could be developed from the envelope according to mathematical principles.

The structural engineers made use of a graphic idea to solve this. They imagined the twisted volume extruded from an ellipse as a cake which, starting from its centre (all the centres of the ellipses are positioned vertically above each other), is divided into equal-sized pieces. The ensuing curved edges along the backs of the pieces of cake generate lines with a defined geometry. Columns could be positioned at these points to follow this line exactly. Consequently, the column structure would not have to follow the twisting envelope, but instead could be designed as a group of single-curvature columns seemingly clinging to the envelope.

Four numbers to describe the design

The geometry of the design could now be described by four numbers: the minor and major axes of the ellipse (R1 = 10 m, R2 = 17.30 m), the number of columns (n = 16) – as with a spoked wheel, the angle between the spokes, and hence the angle of rotation of the columns (whose axes all point towards the centre), is given (360°/16 = 22.5°) – and the vertical spacing of the ellipses (6.40 m). Using these figures it was possible to build a wire mesh model from which all the other dimensions could be derived.

Iterative convergence on the numerical model

The structural engineers employed a 3D framework design programme. The main challenge here was applying realistic wind loads to a non-rotationally symmetric structure. The basis for this was a climate report specially for this structure on this site. This resulted in a mean wind speed of 25 m/s at a height of 10 metres and a maximum two-second gust speed of 38 m/s.

The engineers considered the effects of these wind loads on their framework from eight wind directions and attempted to estimate the preliminary deformations realistically for their calculations according to second-order theory. Using the ensuing member dimensions, specialists then carried out wind tunnel tests on a 1:75 scale 3D model with wind flows from those same eight directions in order to check the assumptions and calculations. The differences between the results were analysed and the framework model modified in such a way that the numerical model and the tests agreed.

The design of the column cross-sections

In every case the highest loads on the columns were on the minor ellipse radii. As the tower twists, so these migrate to the most slender positions. As the column loads decrease from bottom to top, the loads governing the design of the column cross-sections occur right at the bottom, between the pinned bases and the first 'ellipse apexes'.

To keep the construction uniform, all the columns have a constant cross-section measuring 32 × 144 cm. However, depending on the structural requirements, different glulam strength grades are used: GL28c, GL28h, and GL32h.

Steel members for stability

The stability of the twisting tower structure is guaranteed by the ten ellipses, which are fitted between the columns as curved steel box segments, with rigid connections to the columns, and eighty diagonal braces made of steel circular hollow sections. The bracing is only required in areas with higher stresses, i.e. in the areas of the minor ellipse radii, which means that four diagonals are installed here each time. Basically, there are eight long trusses that run diagonally from top to bottom.

Detailed design and prefabrication with millimetre precision

The timber contractor had to work to very tight tolerances during the detailed design of the timber structure and when preparing CNC drawings for the machining work. To ensure optimum load transfer, the H-shaped steel components and bolts with internal threads were glued into the timber sections with epoxy resin. The timber engineers developed an exact 3D computer model that included all geometries plus all cut-outs for connecting plates and other fasteners. The model formed the basis for the CNC machining of all timber and steel components.

Dividing the 65 metre high columns into three parts – two pieces 26 metres long plus one 13 metres long – also evolved out of the structural engineers' erection concept. Contrasting with what an observer might believe at first glance, the sixteen columns are not all different; instead, the simple symmetrical design means every column occurs twice, i.e. there are 'only' eight different column types. However, dividing the columns into three unequal parts resulted in forty-eight separate pieces (thirty-two long and sixteen short segments), which were, indeed, all unique.

Phased column erection

Phase one of the erection concept involved erecting alternate long (26 m) and short (13 m) column segments so that as work proceeded upwards, each higher column segment could be used to assist erection.

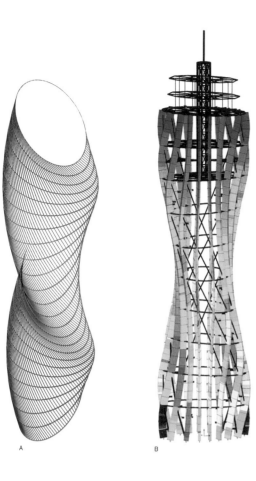

A

B

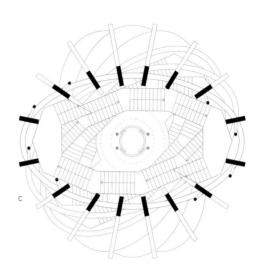

C

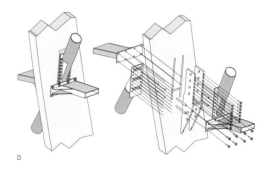

D

E

F

A → Underlying idea: imagine a stack of elliptical cards twisted over its height.

B → An isometric view of the 3D framework with the different stress states of the glulam cross-sections shown in different colours. Red indicates the highest stresses.

C → Horizontal section through the tower at 38.86 metres showing the elliptical levels below, each one turned through the same angle. All column axes point towards the centre.

D + E → Thanks to exactly designed details and perfect CNC machining for assembly, all connectors were able to be installed exactly and all components joined together, without force, on site.

F → Cut-outs in the timber were machined accurately with just 5 millimetre play. Once the steel components were fitted in place, this 'gap' was filled with epoxy resin.

The bottom column segments were guyed back until all the bottommost segments and the steel sections forming the first two ellipses with their diagonal bracing had been erected to form a stable structure. Owing to the height, guying was not possible during the two subsequent erection phases. However, the alternating long/short arrangement allowed the column segments of the next erection phase – involving exclusively long segments – to be braced against the neighbouring, higher segments in each case. During the final column erection phase, long and short column segments were again erected alternately on the existing column sections below so that in the end all columns were the same height.

Fifty-year design life and sound fire protection concept

The tower is designed to last fifty years. Protecting the timber was therefore a key topic for the structural engineers even at the draft design stage. Details at the connections were designed bearing in mind optimum protection for the timber.

Although Eurocode 5 does not permit the building of timber structures with glued joints which are exposed to the weather (service class 3), the structural engineers were able to comply with the code by adding a 15 millimetre allowance to the dimensions required for the column cross-section and declare this as an enclosing or protective layer around the load-bearing core. The timber structure itself is therefore only loaded to 70 per cent of its capacity.

All connections between the glulam columns and elliptical elements and diagonal bracing include a gap so that no moisture can collect and the connections can dry out at all times. As the fasteners are glued into the timber, this results in a type of sealing that prevents water entering the timber and further protects the wood. The downward bevels at the joints between the column segments also help to ensure that the connections remain dry.

The authorities also required a sound fire protection concept for the tower. In the event of a fire, the stability of the tower must be guaranteed until all persons have been evacuated. At the same time, fire and smoke should not spread to such an extent that escaping safely from the tower becomes impossible. The structural requirements guarantee a fire resistance of 90 minutes. Two escape stairs are provided. Fire and smoke compartmentation prevents the spread of fire. If required, 300 m³ of extinguishing water can be sprayed via the sprinkler installation. In addition there is a lightning protection system, emergency lighting, emergency power supply, emergency lift, fire detectors and alarms plus CCTV installed throughout the tower. sjf

A → Zip-like erection concept

B → The 'Skybox' just below 57.60 metres is protected from the weather. The actual structure is 64 metres high. However, above that there are two open viewing platforms each 3.20 metres high.

C → Alternating short and long column segments in the first erection phase. The different lengths enabled the subsequent erection phases to continue similarly so that the higher column sections could be used to stabilise the other sections as they were erected.

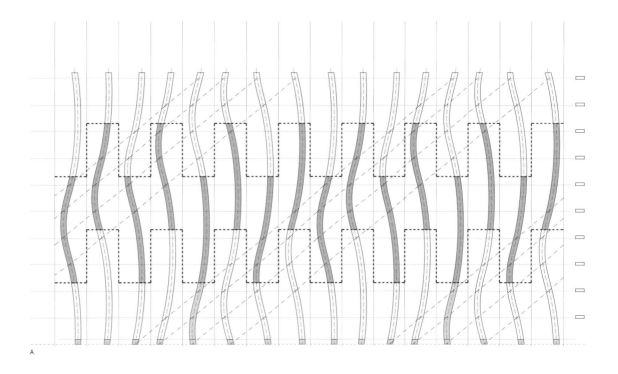

A

B

C

Project Timber viewing tower on Pyramidenkogel mountain
in Keutschach am See (Carinthia), Austria

Form of construction Engineered timber-and-steel structure

Construction period October 2012 to June 2013
(including two months for tower structure)

Costs approx. €8 million (excl. tax)

Gross floor area 700 m²

Client Pyramidenkogel Infrastruktur GmbH & Co. KG, 9020 Klagenfurt,
Austria, www.pyramidenkogel-ktn.at

Project management Kastner ZT-GmbH, 9020 Klagenfurt, Austria,
www.kastner-zt.eu

Architecture Klaura + Kaden + Partner ZT GmbH, 9020 Klagenfurt,
Austria; Architect Mag. Markus Klaura, www.klaura.at,; Architect Mag.
Dietmar Kaden, www.kaden.cc,; Architect Dipl.-Ing. Erich Laure,
www.arch-laure.at

Structural engineering Lackner & Raml ZT GmbH
Dipl.-Ing. Markus Lackner, 9500 Villach, Austria, www.lackner-raml.at

Structural checking services Création Holz GmbH, 9101 Herisau,
Switzerland, www.creation-holz.ch, and Rubner Holzbau GmbH,
3200 Ober-Grafendorf, Austria, www.rubner.com

Wind tunnel tests Wacker Ingenieure, 75217 Birkenfeld, Germany,
www.wacker-ingenieure.de

Timber contractor (fabrication drawings & production)
Rubner Holzbau GmbH, 3200 Ober-Grafendorf (Villach branch),
and 9584 Finkenstein, Austria (project management + erection),
www.rubner.com

Steelwork contractor (fabrication drawings & production)
Zeman & Co GmbH, 1120 Vienna, Austria, www.zeman-stahl.com

Quantity of timber used 600 m³

Carbon (C) content 150 t

Sequestered CO_2 550 t

Further information Time-lapse film of tower construction:
http://tinyurl.com/k6j3fru

Something's moving!

Germany's second wildlife overpass in timber – over the B101 trunk road near Luckenwalde – has been in place since 2012. Its design is based on a tried-and-tested pilot project dating from 2004, the wildlife crossing over the B96 trunk road. This bridge could become a model for others that are to be built right across the country to reconnect natural habitats.

Besides the two motorways, the A9 and the A13, the B101 trunk road is the most important link between Berlin and southern Brandenburg. To promote economic development in the towns and communities of this area, trunk and rural roads fill in the gaps between the widely spaced motorways. The section of the B101 between Luckenwalde and the motorway junction at Ludwigsfelde was widened to four lanes to help channel traffic flows. And a wildlife overpass has crossed the carriageway at Luckenwalde since August 2012.

Wildlife crossings protect people and animals

Wildlife overpasses are soil-covered, landscaped structures that wild animals, especially deer and boars, can use to cross roads safely. They ensure that when roads slice through natural habitats, wild animals, which follow certain routes to their mating grounds in other territories, are not cut off from those areas. Without safe crossing places, wild animals crossing roads represent a very serious danger for road users and the animals themselves.

Considering the many accidents involving wild animals and the associated fatalities, nature conservationists and the roadbuilding authorities in the meantime agree that many more safe crossings must be built to reunite natural habitats.

Timber – the future norm?

Most of the wildlife overpasses built so far in Germany have used concrete or steel-concrete composite construction; only two overpasses are in timber, with a third one approved just recently. One of those overpasses, completed in 2004, is at Wilmshagen, southeast of Stralsund, and crosses the B96, the main road to the Island of Rügen. For a long time it was Germany's – and perhaps the world's – only wildlife overpass in timber. The other overpass has been in use since the summer of 2012 on the B101 at Luckenwalde. It is based on the design principles of the first overpass. After being in use for several years, these principles have proved their worth.

Both structures were developed and supervised by DEGES (Deutsche Einheit Fernstraßenplanungs- und -bau GmbH) on behalf of the national government and the federal states of Mecklenburg-Western Pomerania and Brandenburg.

Saving lives: the wildlife crossing over the B101 trunk road is the second timber bridge in Germany built to enable wild animals to cross a busy road.

A

B

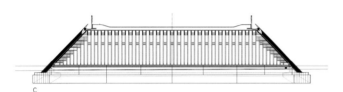

C

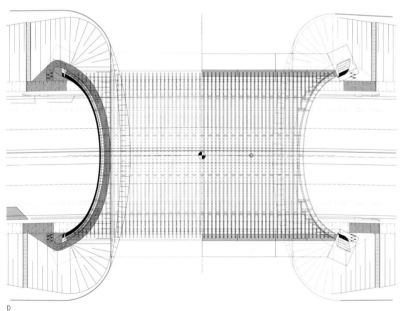

D

Composition of wildlife overpass:
- RSM 7.2.2 standard seed mixture
- 30 cm topsoil
- 15 cm mineral substrate (crest only)
- Coarse soil to ZTVE-StB 09 directive
- Distribution plate
- Geogrid
- Stainless steel mesh to protect against rodents
- Separating membrane (filter) made from rotproof polyethylene
- Drainage blanket
- Separating membrane (filter) made from rotproof polyethylene
- Protective and drainage layer
- Root barrier with protective layer, bitumen-resistant, rhizome-resistant,
  FLL-approved, slate granules to top side
- Felt-torched polymer-modified bitumen sheeting, 2 layers
- Separating membrane (filter) made from rotproof polyethylene
- Felt-torched polymer-modified bitumen sheeting
- Inertol bonding coat
- 14.2 cm CLT
- 20 × 100 cm glulam arch, grade GL28h, larch, e = 80 cm

A → Computer graphic of the primary structure in timber on concrete abutments in the form of strip footings

B → The panels between the final vertical arch and the sloping portal arch were completed with arch segments and transverse members.

C → Longitudinal section

D → Plan

E → Section

E

The remarkable thing about this second wildlife overpass was the requirement to build it in timber – a request from the local council which reached DEGES via the Infra-structure & Agriculture Ministry responsible. The council had heard about the pilot project in Wilmshagen and was impressed by the synthesis of function, form, and material achieved for the first time in that project.

Timber triumphs when comparing different versions
In advance of the tender, DEGES drew up a comparison between a reinforced concrete frame and a three-pin arch in timber, with the following outcome: 'For technical, functional and economic reasons, a timber design is to be preferred.'

Besides the aspects of construction, costs, and design, it was primarily the fast erection that favoured timber, as the bridge had to be built over a busy road. Wood also has two other advantages: any structural components damaged by fire are relatively easy to replace and the same is true for any mechanical damage to the structure caused by road accidents. Further arguments in favour of timber were its better life cycle assessment and the landscaping effect of this renewable building material.

The good durability of the pilot project in Wilms-hagen also convinced the decision-makers, despite the slightly higher cost of maintenance when compared with concrete. One piece of evidence came from an exam-ination of the wood's moisture content in October 2011: at a depth of 4 centimetres the moisture content was between 13.4 and 15.3 per cent, which complies with service class 2 to DIN 1052.

Therefore, DEGES could draw up the design for the new wildlife crossing similarly to the first one and issue a pan-European tender.

Wildlife overpasses must be designed differently to road bridges
The main difference between a wildlife overpass and a road bridge is the lower imposed loads for the former. However, they can be designed for vehicle loads as well in isolated cases. The design guidelines vary to suit the different uses. The specific provisions that must be considered when designing wildlife crossings are as follows:
- The crossing must be located on one of the main routes used by the animals. This requires appropriate studies to be undertaken unless special maps are already available.
- The shape of the land must be such that it is accepted by the wild animals as a crossing.
- According to the recommendations published in Germany for wildlife crossings, the usable width on the crest of the bridge should be 50 metres on

average, but this can be reduced to 40 metres for a constricted crest section.
- Particular attention should be paid to planting, visual screening, noise control, and safety fences. Light and sound barriers should be at least 2 metres high and broaden out like wing walls on both sides of the bridge.
- Vegetation along the fences and on the overpass itself depends on the depths needed for the roots. At the crest the soil covering and potential root depth should be about 50 centimetres. This quickly becomes considerably deeper as we approach the abutments.

The arch – the optimum structure
As with the first wildlife overpass, the designers opted for a three-pin arch of larch glued laminated timber for the main structure to this new, almost 40 metre long crossing (grade GL28h; edge beam: GL24h). But con-trasting with the first crossing, the design does not employ the classical compression arch with a single radius, but a three-centred arch with radii of $R1 = 9.55$ metres, $R2 = 19.35$ metres, and $R3 = 33.50$ metres. In this type of arch the curvature increases towards the abutments. That is an advantage for the clearance needed for road traffic and for the flow of forces in the structure.

The 100 cm deep × 20 cm wide glulam arch members span about 32 metres with a maximum headroom of 7.50 metres. Steel hinges at the abutments and the ridge form the structural system. Spaced at 80 centimetres centre-to-centre, the row of arches forms a sort of tunnel.

At the portals the arches lean inwards at 45 degrees. The panels behind the portal arches are closed off with appropriate arch segments and transverse members. Inclining the portal arches at this angle results in good illumination in the 'tube' and also enables the con-struction of stable embankments.

Curved cross-laminated timber (CLT) panels 142 millimetres thick form the secondary structure. These panels cover the arches and are fixed to them from above with countersunk-head stainless steel screws. The plate effect of this 'sheathing' stabilises the entire system in the transverse direction. The curved shell also carries the load of the soil (up to about 130 kN/m²) and transfers it to the arches.

Erection from centre of structure outwards
Once the reinforced concrete foundations and substruc-ture plus all anchorage points had been completed, the erection of the entire prefabricated timber structure took just four days – spread over two weekends. The busy B 101 was therefore closed completely for only a very short time. Further work on the crossing was carried

out with traffic flowing, with just single carriageways having to be cordoned off temporarily.

For stability, also during transport and erection, pairs of half-frames were joined with 100 centimetre deep × 20 centimetre wide struts (b=24 cm, or 28 cm behind the portal arches) using continuous threaded bars to form pairs of half-arches. Erection proceeded outwards from the centre of the structure using four mobile cranes. Opposite pairs of half-arches were first attached to the abutments and then lowered to meet at the ridge.

The CLT panels were curved to fit the different curvature of the glulam arches exactly depending on their position on the arch. The infill members behind the portal arches were also factory-prefabricated. However, the Accoya wood cladding to those arches was attached on site. The cladding includes several inspection hatches so that the condition of the structure underneath can be checked at any time.

One special feature is the edge detail around the portal with beams measuring 40 × 40 cm, which are in double curvature owing to the angle of the portal arches.

Absolutely crucial: protection against moisture

To protect against moisture, special, multi-layer water-proofing consisting of felt-torched bitumen sheeting was laid on the CLT shell. This is supplemented by drainage along the line of the springings to prevent a build-up of water, ingenious construction measures to control moisture and a root barrier. Continuous moisture monitoring ensures that any leaks can be tackled immediately.

The timber structure was given a coat of clear varnish, which also protects against water splashed up from the road. However, the natural ventilation ensures that splashing water dries out quickly and so protects against changing moisture levels caused by passing traffic. Splashes of de-icing salt even have a preservative effect.

Soil-covered timber structure

Once the structure was finished, the whole area was covered in soil ready for planting grass, shrubs, and bushes; some 70 centimetres of soil were tipped on the crest, 7 metres above the abutments. The designers have provided 2 metre high light and sound barriers on the structure and along the B 101.

When it comes to wildlife overpasses, the dead load of the structure plays a subsidiary role compared with pedestrian and road bridges, although even here, timber offers advantages, e.g. the low load on the subsoil.

Timber bridge-building has developed very positively over the past ten years and renders possible the construction of durable bridges. Wildlife overpasses in timber offer the chance of combining ecological goals with good looks. sjf

A

B

A → The special waterproof finish was applied on site. The edge beam in double curvature is readily visible in this photo.

B → The Accoya wood cladding to the portal arches was also attached on site.

C → Four mobile cranes were used to erect the pairs of half-arches.

D → The half-arches were first attached to the abutments and then lowered into position for connection at the ridge to form a complete arch.

E → The designers established that the most economic structure would be a barrel vault of three-centred arches in glulam combined with a decking of cross-laminated timber as the secondary structure. This is the shortest path for transferring loads from the covering of soil to the abutments.

C

Project **Wildlife overpass in timber near Luckenwalde**

Form of construction **Soil-covered arch structure made of larch glulam, with CLT sheathing and special multi-layer waterproofing; reinforced concrete foundations and abutments**

Construction period, substructure **5 weeks per abutment side**

Construction period, superstructure **February to October 2012 (incl. prefabrication of timber arches, earthworks, and light and sound barriers)**

Completed **2012**

Costs **€3 million, made up of €300 000 for concrete works (foundations, abutments) and €2.7 million for timber structure, soil covering, and protective screens**

Client **DEGES – Deutsche Einheit Fernstraßenplanungs- und -bau GmbH, 10117 Berlin, Germany, www.deges.de, on behalf of the national government and the federal states of Brandenburg and Mecklenburg-Western Pomerania**

Structural engineering **Schwesig + Lindschulte GmbH, 18055 Rostock, Germany, www.lindschulte.de**

Checking engineers **Blaß & Eberhart, 76227 Karlsruhe, Germany, www.ing-bue.de**

Timber works, project management & construction **Schaffitzel Holz-industrie GmbH + Co. KG, 74523 Schwäbisch Hall, Germany, www.schaffitzel.de; Schaffitzel+Miebach, Faszination Brücken GmbH, 53797 Lohmar, Germany, www.schaffitzel-miebach.com**

Concrete works (foundations, abutments) **ARIKON/DIW consortium**

Quantity of timber used **approx. 680 m³**

Carbon (C) content **170 t**

Sequestered CO_2 **623 t**

Length (of 'tunnel') at crest **38.90 m**

Span between abutments **32 m**

Crossing area **1245 m²**

Larch glulam, GL28h **approx. 506 m³**

Larch glulam, GL24h **approx. 13.5 m³**

Spruce CLT **approx. 1820 m² (or approx. 158.44 m³)**

Accoya facade sections **approx. 100 m²**

Steel components **approx. 70.5 t**

Reinforced concrete (foundations) **1060 m³**

Light and sound barriers **approx. 680 m²**

Earthworks **approx. 27 000 m³**

D

E

Oslo International Airport sets new standards

A new terminal and pier have been added to the major international airport serving Norway's capital. The architecture to passive-house standard with load-bearing structures made of glued laminated timber with exceptional dimensions and designs is just as pioneering as the energy concept, which uses snow for cooling!

More than 6 billion euros are to be invested in the expansion and modernisation of Norway's airport infrastructure by 2029, with about 1.7 billion euros of that being spent on Oslo International Airport. The expansion project will enable the airport's annual capacity to be raised from the current figure of 24.2 million passengers to 28 million. Important aspects for the architects and planning team were ensuring that the overall airport upgrade, consisting of several individual projects, could be accomplished without interfering with each other, without interrupting airport operations, and completed on time, with passenger numbers already increasing steadily. This economic factor was the main reason behind the decision to use modern timber construction with a high degree of prefabrication for many parts of the expansion project.

Duty-free shops as economic factor

The constant growth in numbers of passengers even during the expansion phase is expected to lead to an increase in revenue amounting to about 500 million euros – a figure that must be secured. Duty-free shops, restaurants, cafés, and parking charges are responsible for much of this increase in the airport's revenue. The expansion project will double the space available for these high-yield commercial factors from the current $10\,800\,m^2$ to about $20\,000\,m^2$. The construction project comprises the modernisation and modification of the internal and external circulation routes plus the erection of three large buildings: a new inter-city railway station, a second terminal with arrival and check-in areas, and a third pier with eleven additional jet bridges. As Norway now prefers to use the renewable raw material wood for public-sector building projects, the roof structures to the three buildings will be or were built using glued laminated timber, whereas the roof to the new Pir Nord will be clad with Swedish oak slats.

'Zero-tolerance' quality standard

Glued laminated timber (glulam) is made from thin laminations joined lengthwise with glued structural finger joints. The individual laminations are stacked and fastened together with adhesive over their whole area under high pressure to form compact building components. Individual laminations can be bent prior to joining with adhesive, which enables the fabrication of curved beams.

The highly advanced technical development enables great lengths and large cross-sections to be produced with essentially unlimited forms, which makes glulam

How Oslo International Airport will look after the current expansion works are completed in April 2017, with the second terminal (right of centre) and additional pier (foreground).

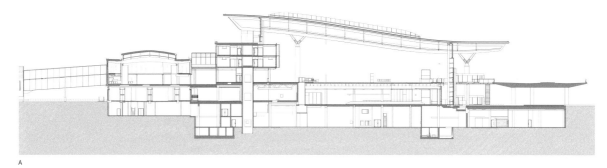

A

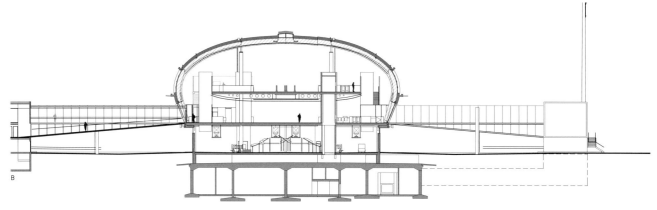

B

C

A → Section through new Sentralbygg Vest terminal

B → Section through new Pir Nord

C → Aircraft and architecture consummated in a structural, functional, and artistic form: the wing-like glulam beams to the new terminal cantilever beyond the building envelope

beams ideal for the long spans of single-storey sheds and bridges. The prefabrication of the glulam beams with millimetre precision for Oslo Airport had to meet the very highest quality standards and be produced and delivered on time according to a so-called zero-tolerance policy that had been prescribed by the client. One outcome of that policy was the need for large production buildings so that work could continue regardless of the weather. That was a key criterion for the award of the contract, which the German company W. u. J. Derix / Poppensieker & Derix was able to fulfil. They subsequently supplied the load-bearing structures for the airport made of FSC- or PEFC-approved wood. This glued laminated timber company has two plants and two production lines that can process components up to 65 metres long – a figure that could well be a record, not only in Europe.

Accurate and on time

The glulam beams were produced in a fully automated, computer-controlled design and fabrication process. The design data from the timber engineer's 3D design programme were sent directly to the CNC production lines with their laser technology. All the machining of the glued laminated timber, including longitudinal, diagonal, and mitre cuts, drilling, and machining of contours at all angles, takes place on the CNC production lines. Even large cross-sections can be fabricated in one process on the highly accurate, five-axis machines, which can carry out three-dimensional machining operations as well. This process also included the various slots in different sizes required in the Oslo project for connections and joints with steel dowels and steel plates at the load-bearing nodes. Owing to the large number of large components that had to be glued, W. u. J. Derix / Poppensieker & Derix developed their own press specially for the airport project in order to comply with the specified quality standard and the deadlines. Finally, all glulam components were transported 1300 kilometres to the building site on time.

Glulam / reinforced concrete hybrid design

As with the first terminal, the architecture of the load-bearing structure for the new passenger check-in building, Sentralbygning Vest, is based on a glulam / reinforced concrete hybrid design. The new rectangular building, measuring 126 metres long and 95 metres wide, is directly alongside the first terminal. Seven pairs of clad glulam trusses supported on circular reinforced concrete columns 54 metres apart on each of the main grid-lines form the primary structure. At the airside end the trusses cantilever an impressive 23 metres, at the landside end a more modest 13.65 metres. Sturdy steel arms 3 metres apart on top of the reinforced

concrete columns support the pairs of glulam trusses at a height of 18.80 or 12.80 metres. The long cantilevers, curving over their length and with an elegant taper at the end, awaken associations with the huge wings of intercontinental aircraft and seem to fulfil their structural task here with consummate ease. The dimensions of their top and bottom chords, laid up in parallel blocks, speak for themselves: 89 centimetres wide and 53 centimetres deep (top), 73 centimetres wide and 105 centimetres deep (bottom). Whereas the top chords were clad, the finely sanded surfaces of the bottom chords were left exposed. Between these main beams, 2.50 metre deep glulam trusses 6 metres apart and spanning about 15 metres constitute the symmetrical secondary structure.

Arches for pier

The roof structure for the new terminal consists of a total of 138 primary and secondary glulam trusses that were prefabricated in Germany and then delivered to Norway just in time. Sentralbygning Vest covers an area of about 12 000 m², although the multi-storey internal fitting-out will result in a final usable floor area of 52 000 m². The new Pir Nord for the jet bridges is 320 metres long and has an area of 63 000 m². Its fan-like shape reminds the observer of a giant jet engine.

At its junction with Terminal 1, the pier is 120 metres wide, but gradually tapers towards the airfield. After about 160 metres it merges with a symmetrical tube 46 metres wide and 16 metres high, whose load-bearing structure consists of 28 arches made of pairs of glulam sections. Owing to the taper, the structures on the first eleven main grid-lines differ in size, whereas the structures on the remaining seventeen grid-lines of the tube are identical. There are pairs of glulam arches 32 centimetres apart with cross-sections between 28 × 120 and 28 × 250 centimetres on every main grid-line. The longest individual glulam segments of the arches, with steel plates let into the timber to create rigid splices, are an impressive 47 metres long.

Passive-house standard for terminal

From 2015 onwards, all new buildings in Norway must be built to the passive-house energy standard. Accordingly, at least 50 per cent of the heating energy requirement must be provided by renewable energy sources. Compared with the annual figure for the existing Terminal 1 (490 kWh/m²), the primary energy requirement for heating and cooling in the new Sentralbygning Vest Terminal is to be cut by half. The climate-neutral energy supply to the airport is based on a modular principle. Geothermal energy is one component in this. Two wells extract water from a large body of groundwater beneath the airport and send the water via submersible motors to heat pumps, which extract the energy through compression to supply either the low-energy under-floor heating or the cooling circuits. The two well circuits operate separately. In the first one, relatively cold water, compared with the outside temperature, is pumped to the surface in summer and re-injected in winter. In the second one, relatively warm water, compared with the outside temperature, is pumped to the surface in winter and re-injected in summer. This method balances out the groundwater reservoir in terms of the quantity of water and its temperature.

Heat from waste water, snow for cooling in summer
Another component in the energy supply is the use of the airport's waste water. First of all, a sewage treatment plant cleans the waste water. In a second stage, a heat recovery system with heat exchanger extracts the waste heat from the treated waste water. After that, this heat is fed back into some of the treated waste

water and fed via a pipeline to the airport's heat pump stations at a temperature of 10 to 16°C.

The summer cooling system for Pir Nord is unique. In winter, snow with a total volume of 90 000 m³ is collected and piled up in a 30 000 m³ basin, then covered with sawdust and chippings to insulate it and thus slow down the melting process in the summer. Like a glacier, the meltwater gradually seeps through the mass of snow. On the floor of the basin, the water, with a temper-ature just above 0°C, is collected and fed to a heat exchanger. This extracts the energy from the meltwater and feeds this to the cooling and ventilation systems in the new pier. Afterwards, the water is fed back to the basin so the snow-cooling system can be recharged to a certain extent and keep the process going. By using a local resource, in this case snow, it was possible to install a much smaller conventional ventilation system, which should only be needed as a backup or to cover peak loads. In addition, this solves the problem of large amounts of snow at Oslo International Airport in the future. mwl

Client Avinor AS and Oslo Lufthavn AS, 2061 Gardermoen, Norway, www.avinor.no

Architecture Nordic Office of Architecture, 0306 Oslo, Norway, www.nordicarch.com; Cowi AS, 2800 Kongens Lyngby, Denmark, www.cowi.com; Norconsult AS, 1338 Sandvika, Norway, www.norconsult.no; Aas-Jakobsen AS, 7037 Trondheim, Norway, www.aas-jakobsen.no; Per Rasmussen AS, 1313 Vøyenenga, Norway, www.ipras.no

Project management ÅF Advansia AS, 1366 Lysaker, Norway, www.afconsult.com

Contractor, roof structure Kruse Smith AS, 4630 Kristiansand, Norway, www.kruse-smith.no

Structural engineers Sweco Norge AS, 0212 Oslo, Norway, www.sweco.no

Glulam structures W. u. J. Derix GmbH & Co., 41372 Niederkrüchten, Germany; Poppensieker & Derix GmbH & Co. KG, 49492 Westerkappeln, Germany, www.derix.de

Steel components & connectors Brüninghoff GmbH & Co. KG, 46359 Heiden, Germany, www.brueninghoff.de

Transportation of glulam members Ernst Laumeyer GmbH, 49492 Westerkappeln, Germany, www.laumeyer.de

Start on site 2011

Scheduled completion April 2017

Total costs €1.7 billion

Quantity of timber used 3500 m³

Carbon (C) content 875 t

Sequestered CO_2 3208 t

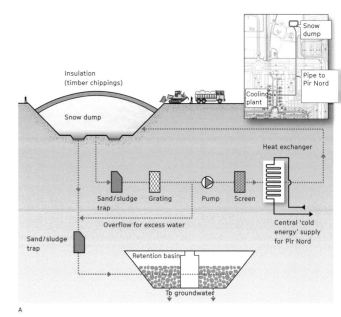

A

A → Unique – and not just when it comes to international airports: cold water for the air-conditioning and ventilation systems in Pir Nord is reclaimed from a basin that stores snow!

B → Timber construction in the 21st century: glulam beams prefabricated with millimetre precision and transported more than 1300 kilometres to arrive just in time

C → Arches form the load-bearing structure to the new Pir Nord.

D → The modern load-bearing structure of the terminal consists of timber, steel, and concrete. The top and bottom chords of the trusses are glulam components laid up in parallel blocks. Trusses are also used for the secondary structure.

E → The unusual glued laminated timber roof beams for the Sentralbygg Vest passenger check-in building span 90 metres between reinforced concrete columns.

B

C

D

E

Picture credits

Cover Wolfram Kübler. **Introduction** 8, 11 A, D, E: Museum Niesky. 11 B: Baukunstarchiv, Berlin. 11 C: Baukunstarchiv, Berlin / Karsten, William F. 14 A, B: Fam. Ohnesorge / Archiv Prof. Wolfgang Rug. 15 C: Markus Bollen Photography. 15 D: Schmees & Lühn. **WIPO conference hall, Geneva** 18: David Matthiessen. 21 A, B: schlaich bergermann und partner. 21 C, 22 A, 23 B: Charpente Concept. 21 D: David Matthiessen. 23 C, E: Dasta Charpentes Bois / Gilbert Buron. 23 D: Charpente Concept / Lucien Fortunati. 24 A, B: Behnisch Architekten. 25, C: David Matthiessen. **Elephant house, Zurich** 26, 29 A: Jean-Luc Grossmann. 29 B-E, 30 B, 32 C, 33 E, F: Walt+Galmarini. 30 A, C, 32 A, D: Markus Schietsch Architekten GmbH. 32 B: MERK Timber GmbH. 33 G: Sika AG, Ricardo Gomez. **G3 Shopping Resort, Gerasdorf** 36: ATP/Kurt Kuball. 38 A, 40 A-D, 41 E-G, J: Graf-Holztechnik GmbH. 38 B, D, E: ATP Architekten und Ingenieure. 38 C: ATP/Kurt Kuball. 41 H, I: Hannes Plackner / Holzkurier. **Warehouse, Philippsburg** 42, 44 C, 47 D, E: Brigida González. 44 A, B, 46 A: gumpp . heigl . schmitt. 46 B, C: Lignatur AG. 47 F: Ing.-Büro von Fragstein. **Railway operations centre, Laubenbachmühle** 48, 51 B, C, 52 E, 53 F: Zieser Architekt. 51 A, 52 B-D: Rubner Holzbau AG. 52 A: NÖVOG/Bleuer. **Organic supermarket, Windhof** 54, 57 C, 59 C: Nikos Welter. 57 A, B, 58 A, B: hainarchitektur. **Casa Salute, Margreid** 60, 63 A-C, 64 A, 65 C: Casa Salute S.r.l.. 63 D, 65 B: Studio M7/Architekt Marco Sette. **Sports hall, Sargans** 68, 70 B, C, 71 H, 73: Roman Keller, Zürich. 70 A, 71 I, J: blue architects AG. 70 D: Walt+Galmarini, 70 E-G: Susanne Jacob-Freitag. **Indoor rollerblade arena, Geisingen** 74, 76 B, 79 E: G.R. Wett, CENTRAPLAN Architekten. 76 A, C, D: WIEHAG GmbH/ kw-holz. 78 A, B, 79 D: Jochen Hummel / Wiehag. 78 C: Uhrig. 79 F: Isaak Papadopoulos. **Acquaworld, Concorezzo** 80, 83 C, D: Sering Srl / Bluwater Spa. 84 A: Sering Srl. 83 A, B, 85 B-D: Rubner Holzbau AG. **Les Thermes, Strassen** 86, 91 D: GEGENPOL. 89 A: Ochs GmbH. 89 B, C, 90 A, B, 91 C: Hermann & Valentiny et Associés. **Multifunction stadium, Nice** 92, 96 A, 98 B, 99 C: Allianz Riviera / Milène Servelle. 95 B, 98 A: Allianz Riviera. 95 A, C: Wilmotte & Associés. 97 B: Fargeot LC. 97 C, D: VINCI/ F. Vigouroux. **LCT One, Dornbirn, and IZM, Montafon** 102: Norman A. Müller. 105 A-E, 106 B, 108 A-C: Architekten Hermann Kaufmann ZT GmbH. 106, 108 D, E: Bruno Klomfar. **Apartment building, Wagramer Straße, Vienna** 110, 114 A-C, 115 D, E: Bruno Klomfar. 112 A-C: schluder architektur ZT GmbH. **Canols staff hostel, Lenzerheide** 116, 119 B, 121 A-D: Lenz, Voneschen & Partner AG. 119 A: Dominik Sutter. 119 C: Graubünden Holz. **Wälderhaus, Hamburg** 122, 125 A-C, 126 A: Bernadette Grimmenstein. 126 B, C: Studio Andreas Heller Architects & Designers. 126 D: Heinrich Haveloh GmbH. **Woodcube, Hamburg** 128, 131 A, B: Bernadette Grimmenstein. 132 A: DeepGreen Development GmbH. 132 B, C: architekturagentur. 133 D-F: IBA Hamburg / Martin Kunze. **c13, Berlin** 136, 139 C, 140 A, 141 C, 143 A: Bernd Borchardt. 139 A, B, 141 B, 143 B: Kaden und Partner Architekten. 143 C: Pirmin Jung Ingenieure für Holzbau. **TM50, Nuremberg** 144, 147 C, D: Peter Dörfel Fotodesign. 147 A, B: DXV Architektur. 149 A: Enis Avdic. 149 B-D: HU-Holzunion GmbH. **Wooden church, Eiterfeld-Unterrufhausen** 152, 155 B: Christian Reinhardt. 155 A, 156 A: Matthias Wald. 156 B: Marc Wilhelm Lennartz. 157 C, D: Norman Heimbrodt Architekt. **Overmeyer organic farm, Seevetal** 158, 160 B, C, 161 E-G, 163 B: Bernadette Grimmenstein. 160 A: Urban Catalyst Studio. 160 D: Scaven Hütz Architekt. 163 A: Meisterkollektiv. **Viewing tower, Pyramidenkogel, Keutschach am See** 164, 167 E, F, 169 A, C: Rubner Holzbau AG. 167, A, C: Klaura Kaden + Partner ZT GmbH. 167 B, D: Lackner & Raml. 169 B: pierer.net. **Wildlife overpass, Luckenwalde** 170, 175 C: DEGES GmbH-Fotodesign Legrand. 172 A, C-E: Schwesig + Lindschulte. 172 B, 175 D, E: DEGES. 174 A, B: Schaffitzel+Miebach. **Airport expansion, Oslo** 176, 180 A: Oslo Lufthavn AS. 178 A, B: Nordic Office of Architecture. 178 C, 181 B-F: W. u. J. Derix / Poppensieker & Derix

The authors

Susanne Jacob-Freitag, Dipl.-Ing., studied construction engineering. For 10 years she was an editor with a German journal for timber construction. Since 2007 she has been working as a freelance journalist, focusing on engineered timber construction and architecture. She runs a business providing editorial services, manu*Scriptur,* in Karlsruhe.

www.manuscriptur.de

Marc Wilhelm Lennartz, Dipl.-Geogr., studied physical and economic geography, urban planning, urban and regional development, transport policy, and soil science at the Rheinische Friedrich Wilhelms University in Bonn. He works as a freelance journalist, consultant, and author specialising in modern (timber) architecture, urban planning, renewable energy, and renewable raw materials.

www.mwl-sapere-aude.com

The Natural Change in Urban Architecture
INVENTED BY RHOMBERG

About Cree GmbH
The name Cree has been borrowed from the Native Americans of
the same name in recognition of their natural way of life, and is also
the abbreviation of Creative Resource & Energy Efficiency; as part
of the internationally renowned Rhomberg Group, it is the logical next
step growing out of four generations of high-rise construction
experience. The company was formed in 2010 and, with its innovative
strategies, wants to create an impetus and spread ideas for the
better use of natural resources. New concepts are designed to reduce
both resource and energy consumption in the life cycle of buildings
and thereby counteract negative changes in the climate. The timber
construction specialist envisions a hybrid timber tower block with
up to 30 storeys and a total height of 100 metres which requires less
energy and fewer resources in its entire life cycle – from the design
through to disposal. The means to this end is the LCT (Life Cycle Tower)
system. With the LCT One office tower in Dornbirn and the Illwerke
Centre in Montafon, Vandans, Cree has now provided two projects as
evidence that the concept functions well under actual working
conditions. In addition a three-storey building was set up with the
LCT-System in the town of Memmingen, Bavaria, for the first time in
a mixed occupancy with offices and penthouse-apartments.
www.creebyrhomberg.com

Translation from German into English: Philip Thrift
Copy editing: John O'Toole
Project management: Alexander Felix, Petra Schmid
Production: Amelie Solbrig
Layout, cover design, and typography: Atelier Landolt / Pfister

Library of Congress Cataloging-in-Publication data
A CIP catalog record for this book has been applied for at the Library
of Congress.

Bibliographic information published by the German National Library
The German National Library lists this publication in the Deutsche
Nationalbibliografie; detailed bibliographic data are available on the
Internet at http://dnb.dnb.de.

This publication is also available as an e-book
(ISBN PDF 978-3-0356-0458-0; ISBN EPUB 978-3-0356-0460-3)
and in a German language edition (ISBN 978-3-0356-0455-9).

© 2016 Birkhäuser Verlag GmbH, Basel
P.O. Box 44, 4009 Basel, Switzerland
Part of Walter de Gruyter GmbH, Berlin/Boston

Printed on acid-free paper produced from chlorine-free pulp. TCF ∞

Printed in Germany

ISBN 978-3-0356-0454-2

9 8 7 6 5 4 3 2 1

www.birkhauser.com